Ennis Richmond

Boyhood

A Plea for Continuity in Education

Ennis Richmond

Boyhood
A Plea for Continuity in Education

ISBN/EAN: 9783337366193

Printed in Europe, USA, Canada, Australia, Japan

Cover: Foto ©Suzi / pixelio.de

More available books at **www.hansebooks.com**

BOYHOOD

A PLEA FOR CONTINUITY IN EDUCATION

BY

ENNIS RICHMOND

LONGMANS, GREEN, AND CO.
39 PATERNOSTER ROW, LONDON
NEW YORK AND BOMBAY
1899

CONTENTS.

INTRODUCTION.

SOME years ago I heard a schoolmaster say that, in his opinion, parents were a clumsy contrivance of Providence for the production of schoolboys. I think that many schoolmasters, especially masters of preparatory schools, are apt to come to the same conclusion. The average parent and the average schoolmaster do not meet on the common ground of sympathy. This is wrong, and the reason of it and why it is wrong I hope to be able to show. In writing as I do, of this want of sympathy which so spoils the joint work of parent and schoolmaster, I should like to say at once that there are hundreds of parents to whom most of what I shall say does not apply. But I am treating, at any rate at first, of the average case. For the average parent to become the ideal parent is by no means

1

impossible. Parents err in this matter from a misconception of the meaning of love, but the love is there. As to the schoolmaster, I am afraid that he has not always such a fair starting-ground. But even here there is to be found such a thing as the best, something better than the average; and it is our duty as parents not to rest content with anything but the best that can be found; and I hope to show why this is necessary if we are to do what we ought for our boys.

An average parent sends his boy to school to be educated in certain branches of head-learning and to learn "to be a man"; an average schoolmaster takes the boy to help towards making an income. No parent really wants to hand over his boy, body and soul, to an entirely new influence, and yet, as a rule, in sending a young boy to school this is practically what he does. What he *wants* to do is to send his boy where he will learn what it is necessary for him to learn in order that he may pass his examinations, and where he will get his angles, moral and physical, rounded off. What the average parent really *does* is to send his boy into an atmosphere which gradually envelops him, which becomes his life, while his home becomes only an episode. The parents instinctively feel this, though they would not acknowledge it, and the consequence is that often there grows up in them a sort of jarring jealousy of the school which is apt to find expression in many ways. During the first year or so of a boy's school life the home ties pull hard enough to make him feel all in sympathy with his home belongings, and he is probably home-sick and not always happy; by degrees, however, this home-sickness wears off because the school influence becomes so strong that the home influence is, to a large extent, submerged. The lad still likes to go home for his holidays, but he comes back to school by no means only because he is obliged to do so; he still loves his parents, but he does not centre in them as he used to do. As I said, school becomes his life, his world.

This is not right, but this is what happens in nine cases out of ten. Parents cannot take in the whole situation as a schoolmaster can; they do not know what "might have been,"

and they try to be content with what *is*. A
schoolmaster sees all kinds of parents and all
kinds of boys; a parent sees only his own boy
or boys and the one schoolmaster to whom he
sends them. A parent cannot enter into com-
parisons as a schoolmaster can, and a schoolmaster is apt to place his one or two "ideal
parents" on a pedestal apart, and contentedly
class all others, as my friend did, as a clumsy
contrivance of Providence for the production
of schoolboys. Many a schoolmaster might be
inclined to put it in this way: "Parents are a
clumsy contrivance for the production of the
wherewithal for making my income"; and I
think that, as a rule, one would find the
average parents concurring in this idea of the
main motive for which men work in a school.
They prefer to acknowledge it. They prefer
to pay as high fees for their boy's education as
they can manage, because they instinctively
feel that the more they pay the more they are
saved the unpleasant feeling that anything is
being done for their children "for love"; they
would wish every service that is rendered to
their boy to be amply rewarded, so that they

should not be laying themselves under any obligation in the receiving of these services. And the schoolmasters feel this, and I think I may say that many a one is very well contented that this should be so ; at the same time, with these men, whose chief motive in taking up educational work is the one that I have implied, any influence which they acquire over the boys in their charge, any direction in which they lead them, must be entirely independent of the home influence, the home direction. Put with this the fact that a boy, after he leaves home for school, spends more than two-thirds of his life away from home, and that when he *is* at home there is, as a rule, very little direct, *continuous* routine or influence, and one can scarcely be surprised that the school influence is the dominant factor in a boy's life. As I said, parents cannot appreciate this with the same force that a schoolmaster can, they have never tried any other way of looking at the matter, and they do not consider what might be the result if other ideas prevailed.

A boy goes to school so unformed in

character that, of course, he bends to the immense pressure that is there brought to bear upon him. As I pointed out, most boys *at first* instinctively resent this influence and are not too happy, even in the best of schools; and this resentment and the consequent home-sickness incline to make a boy's feeling about his school respond to and encourage, in his parents, the natural jealousy of the school, of which I have spoken, until the time comes when the school influence has superseded that of the home, and school becomes the boy's life; then, oddly enough, parents generally accept the inevitable, and are fairly well contented to let their boys drift out of their lives as far as any *real* intercourse goes. Until parents begin to feel that things as they are, are unsatisfactory, both in the working and in the results, one cannot hope for much change; and they are most eminently unsatisfactory, and I am firmly convinced that this need not be the case. I am quite certain that the home influence might be maintained unbroken through everything—school, college, public life. And I am certain of this because

I have seen it in many instances, instances which only serve to emphasise the fact that, in the majority of cases, the influence of home is not what it should be, and what it might be.

Until parents appreciate how immensely strong the influence of school is, and prepare their boys, during their early years at home, to lean upon and draw all their best impulse from home, to *root* in home, it is impossible that the life of school, when the boys get fairly into it, should not absorb and envelop them. And, even with the best preparation at home, the jarring of the spirit of home life and the spirit of school life must obtain, until parents and schoolmasters *work together*. The forces applied to the boy ought to proceed in the same direction and work to the same point. As it is—to use a simple illustration— we have two forces working in different directions applied to a human "particle". At first the forces are equal, and therefore the "particle's" line of journey proceeds at an equal distance from that of each of the forces applied. As the one force (that of school) becomes stronger, the "particle's" line of

journey must approximate more closely to
that of the stronger force. The stronger the
influence of school then, the weaker the
influence of home. We can see how wrong a
conclusion this is. If the two forces worked
in the same direction the whole matter would
be changed. But this cannot be as long
as parents and schoolmasters continue to
be "natural enemies". By this I do not
mean that they do not—apart from the most
important question of all—regard each other
with a kindly and tolerant spirit; or that they
do not treat each other with the courtesy of
well-bred men and women, but the average
case with them stands somewhat thus: A
schoolmaster looks upon boys as useful material
out of which to make a living, and on which to
expend his energy for work, and he regards
the parent as a necessary evil. The parents
look upon schools as the only medium through
which their boys can get what they require in
the preparation of their characters as men, and
they, in their turn, regard the schoolmaster as
a necessary evil.

A schoolmaster knows that, in most cases,

a boy has to be entirely remodelled before he is "fit for a schoolboy"; the parents feel that in sending their boy to school they are handing him over to an influence, to a life they know little of, and make but a slight attempt to appreciate, and they cling desperately to their children's love, and in their efforts to keep it are continually, though often quite unintentionally, attempting to depreciate this new influence of which they are, quite naturally, very jealous. I think that parents and schoolmasters regard each other with much the same sort of feeling as do nurses and governesses, and for much the same reasons; and I think if we look at the matter in the light of this analogy we shall see that this jealousy on the part of parents, this high-handed contempt on the part of schoolmasters, are primitive feelings, instinctive rather than the result of experience. Sad, indeed, would it be if the more we knew of the teacher of our boys the more we disliked and mistrusted him, and equally sad if the more a schoolmaster knew of a parent the greater was his contempt.

And this brings us to half the solution of

the difficulty. It should be the aim of each individual parent to get to know, as intimately as circumstances permit, the character and personality of the man under whom he or she places his or her son. It should be laid far more to heart than it is that the boy is going to spend the greater part of the next few years with this man, and those years—as far as the formation of his manhood goes—the most impressionable years of his life. A mother will take a nurse on the personal recommendation of a friend, with a certain amount of confidence, because her friend has personally known and come into contact with the woman, and yet with not enough confidence for her not to feel it necessary to watch her carefully, to be with her as much as possible until her own confidence in the woman is established. And how often does it not prove that, even with the highest recommendation, the woman is not worthy of confidence ! Why do parents choose a particular school ? Among the best reasons are because it is recommended by a friend, because they know boys who are or have been at the school, because they have heard that the "tone" is good, because of its social standard, or because the place, where the school is, is healthy. All excellent reasons enough, but as nothing compared with the reason which ought to be paramount, that the man under whose care a parent is placing his or her boy, is a man of high character and of noble aims in the education of children. If parents would but feel that in sending their boys to school, especially to a preparatory school, they are sending them to be under the influence of the one man, instead of that they are sending them into a nebulous something called "school," they would take more pains to *know* their boys' schoolmasters, before their boys go to them, and after they are under their charge.

It is an undoubted fact that a very good average school, and a school with a fair "tone," may be kept by a man of no high or noble aims. Up to a certain point a man of this type can keep his school in very fair order, because he knows that people will not send him boys unless he does. From this motive he keeps the boys in good health, from this motive he keeps them up to a certain level of learning, from this motive he endeavours to keep in his school a certain standard of morals and honour; and he does it all with the consciousness that this much he is paid for, and this much he must supply. But this is not the kind of school to which to send our boys if we want to keep a real hold upon them.

In giving above the example of the nurse, I do not mean to say that it is possible to get to know your schoolmaster in the same way that you can get to know your nurse; and, of course, it is not in the least necessary even if it were possible. A schoolmaster is intellectually and socially the equal of the men and women with whom, as parents, he has to deal; and—in all but the most important point of all—one can trust him, as indeed one is obliged to, to work alone, and one would not wish, in any case, to be continually investigating the methods by which a schoolmaster deals with his boys. But the fact remains that far too little care is taken (and this *is* the most important point of all) in ascertaining what is the *character* of the man in whose charge we place our sons, and what are the motives with which he engages in the most important and difficult work that a man can engage in. This carelessness of inquiry must either be due to the fact that we do not really care for our children as we ought; or else it is that parents—at the bottom of their hearts—are not anxious that their boys should be under the influence of any one, whose character and personality are so strong that their own influence over their boys may suffer.

Many parents feel instinctively that in sending their boys away from home they prefer that they should not be under the care of a man who takes very strong views on any point which is likely to have much effect upon their boys' *moral* character and upbringing. The schoolmaster may have strong and original ideas about athletics, how to teach the Latin grammar, cold baths, and so on, and parents take all these kinds of views as quite suitable; they do not affect the home influence. But if there is reason to suppose that a schoolmaster is a man of very strong moral character, of very high aims, and an exalted idea of his work in dealing with the lives of the boys in his care, then parents are apt to be chary of putting their boys into his charge, and if their higher nature forces them to do so, the jealousy, of which I have spoken, very naturally comes to the surface. And all the while this jealousy is entirely misplaced, for if parents would, after selecting their school for all the ordinary reasons, make it their business to find out whether the head of the school is a man who, in the education of boys, cares for and sympathises with all that education really means, in its truest and deepest sense; and if they would decide on no school, except where such a man is to be found at its head, they would find that in working with his boys, the great aim of this man is to work with their parents. If we have the power of sending our boys to be under the charge of such a man, we are wrong indeed to allow selfish jealousy to make us shrink from placing our children where love will be the ruling principle in their education. We would not wish to acknowledge, even to ourselves, that our children might love us less because they are learning to love others;

we would not wish to mistrust the quality of our own love for our children to such an extent that we fear to let others enter the lists against us lest their love should—in doing what we have failed to do—prove a more efficient help to our boys than our own has been.

It is of all truths—as regards schools and schoolmasters—the greatest, that the higher the aim of the schoolmaster the more likely he is to be anxious to work through and with the parents of the boys under his charge ; and for this reason, the higher the moral aim and spirit of the school the stronger will the influence of home remain. The best school in England is the school which, in dealing with its boys, has the highest moral aim, and that school will be one whose boys will learn to love their homes the better the longer they are in that school.

I think parents may say : " This may be all very well ; but how is one to find out whether a man's aims are noble, and whether his moral character is high ? It is easy enough to find out whether the boys at school have cold baths, whether they change for games and so on, but one can't go up to a man and say 'Have you a noble character? Do you work in your school from the highest motives?'" No, but how would it be if we took a humbler line, and told the schoolmaster (remembering always in talking to him that *he* has dealt with hundreds of boys, while we have dealt with only one or two) in what way we had been endeavouring hitherto to bring up our boy in the right way, so that when he left us to go to school he might be able to choose the right and follow the highest? I will tell you, with all confidence, that a schoolmaster who cares for his boys as he should, would respond immediately, and you should find no difficulty in conducting the discussion of your boy's education on a far higher level than that of cold baths, and the changing of flannels, important as these may be.

As a general thing, a parent's visit to a schoolmaster is of the most perfunctory character, and I think that the contempt which is so apt to leaven the feelings of even the best of schoolmasters, for the parents with whom they come in contact, is due to the knowledge that men and women seem to care so little, on the most important point of all, to whom they send their sons. If the schoolmaster to whom you are speaking, with the intention of sending your boy to his school, be a man who—as a schoolmaster—is "worth his salt," he will respect the spirit which prompts the deep inquiry, and immediately respond to it. It should be remembered that any schoolmaster of experience has met and answered many such inquiries, for there are among us many parents who will not send their boys to a school unless they are certain of the moral stamina of the man at the head of it as a trainer of boys. I do not mean to say that the schoolmaster who talks most glibly of sacred things is, of necessity, the man who is the most to be trusted. If we are taken in by the plausibility of the glib schoolmaster, the man who adapts himself to the views of his company, we must, of course, suffer for our mistake. There are plausible men with low aims everywhere and in every profession, and always there are victims to their plausibility. But it is with the usual parent and the usual schoolmaster that I have here to do, leaving aside details

2

which might belong to this or that particular case.

What I want my readers to grasp is this: school influence is immensely strong, and it is the one safeguard of parents to see that this is on the same lines as their own; as a rule it is *not*, simply because parents will not ascertain what is the spirit that rules the life at school; or because—at the bottom of their hearts— they do not wish that it should be the influence of love, which is the only influence which can carry a lad in the same direction as the home influence carries him. The only way by which we can keep our hold on our boys, when they are away from us, is by making sure that we are sending them only where our teaching, and the motives from which we have acted in educating them, are appreciated; and where the spirit with which the work of education is conducted, and the object to be attained, are the same as our own. If we do this, there is no cessation of home influence, though there may be of home life; when our boys return home they find their groove all ready for them and they slip into it quite easily.

One of the great means by which we may keep the influence of home strong and intact through all changes in a boy's life, is by training our boys in such a manner that in their home is their *groove*. While they are away from us we should not allow this groove to get filled up; this is not very easy when one considers how long are their absences, but in the best homes a boy never loses the feeling that, however long he may be away, his place at home is ready for him. Our boys should have their own rooms at home, and, if possible, their own duties, and a boy ought to be expected to keep rules and to live by order in holidays as well as in school-time. Nearly all parents treat their boys in their holidays as though they were doing them a wrong if they do not allow them as much licence as can possibly be managed. If the house be turned upside down and all rules disregarded, if the mother and sisters have to put up with dirt and noise and untidiness, they say : "Oh, it is only for a short time, the boys *must* enjoy their holidays". Parents forget that by this method a boy is learning to treat his home with supreme disrespect. Our boys' holidays are the only time that we have, after they have left us for school, for moulding their characters, for helping them to grow up wise and strong by the influence of our personal contact with them; and yet we allow our boys to behave, all the while that they are with us, with a disregard of our wishes, and of what they know we approve, which can breed in them nothing but selfishness. Boys enjoy their holidays, and love and respect their homes far more when the rules of the household are kept throughout *the year*. I do not mean that some change and relaxation must not, of necessity, be made during our boys' holidays, but no disregard of rules, which leads to laziness, untidiness or self-indulgence should be allowed. Boys are so often selfish and imperious at home because they have learnt to expect that, in their holidays, everything and every one's convenience will give way to their enjoyment. As I said, relaxation there must be, and pleasure there ought to be, but it should be an ordered relaxation, and pleasure which is given *and received* in a proper manner. If this were

so, the rule of school would assist the discipline
of home ; a boy does not need to spend his
holidays in a round of self-indulgence to make
up for the hardships and rigours of term-time ;
he is *quite* happy at school, only it is not such
a good kind of happiness as he gets at home,
because those he loves best are not there.

I said above that I hoped to be able to show
where half the solution of this difficulty of the
antagonism between parent and schoomaster
lay ; and I hope that I may have done so, by
pointing out at some length the great and vital
importance of parent and schoolmaster working together, and by showing that we can only
ensure this by insisting upon having the best
kind of schoolmaster ; the best, that is, in the
sense of a man of the highest character, and
with the highest motives in his dealings with
boys ; in fact—to put it shortly and most truly
—a man who works for love. A man whose
work (meaning his appreciation, in the highest
sense, of the duties which belong to that work)
comes first, and himself and his own personal
advantage, second. But this is only half the
solution. We say that we must have the best

man as schoolmaster, but, to make the solution entire, a schoolmaster must also have the best parent to deal with, and it is our business to see that we are endeavouring to rank as such. Our earliest training of our children leaves sadly much to be desired; we do not aim high enough; we do not prepare our children for the time when they are to leave us; we do not pave the way for the discipline of school, so that when our boys leave us we know that they will obey the rule which they find elsewhere, because they have learnt that good rule is an outward sign of love. We scramble through the first years of our boys' lives with the feeling that once they get to school all our "dirty work" will be done for us. That means nothing more nor less than that we are trusting that the love of others will be more unselfish than our own. We indulge our little boys more than is right, because we feel that the results of this indulgence, the hot temper, the imperious demanding will be dealt with at school. Are we thus to allow another influence than our own to do the work which lays the first foundations of our boys' characters?

Are we thus to lose the opportunity of knitting our boys' hearts to ours by the training and suasion of our love, handing them over for others to do what we will not do for them ourselves? I believe that if, from the birth of our boys, it were our greatest endeavour to keep our eyes fixed upon their ultimate development, regarding school only as our great *help* in building up in our boys such a character as would most tend to perfection, all danger of jealousy on the part of parent, and contempt on the part of schoolmaster, would cease.

Boys do not get a fair start in their homes, the *foundation* of their education is not laid where alone it can be laid as it should be. Parents do not try to gradually bring their boys to the point where they can launch them forth into another life with confidence, with the knowledge that their boys will return to them with no tie loosened which binds them to their home. There is only one way of doing this, and it is no easy way. It is the way of continual care and discipline of our children and of ourselves. Once for all we must realise that on our boy's earliest years depends all the

development of his after life. Boys arrive at
school, as a general thing, quite unfitted for
the life that meets them there, because parents
do not realise the immense importance of early
discipline and training. In the chapters which
follow here I have written from the point of
view of the schoolmaster of very long experience, who has seen what might be, if boys
came to school with a better and truer foundation.

Some years ago Mr. Lyttelton's book,
Mothers and Sons, came into my hands,
and I thought it a very real and practical help.
Quite lately I have read it again. All my life
has been spent with boys; the last five years
of it, as well as many earlier years, with little
boys; and my present comment upon Mr.
Lyttelton's book is, that in no case does he
speak clearly or strongly enough.

I do not propose to make what I am about
to say on this subject of early home training,
from a schoolmaster's point of view, cover the
same ground as does Mr. Lyttelton's book.
His experience is of boys of from fourteen to
eighteen years of age; my most intimate ac-

quaintance is with boys from seven or eight years of age to the age of fourteen, though seven years of my life were spent in dealing with public school boys.

I hope I may prove, in what I say, that though a good school can and will carry on good work begun at home, and though it will build good material on a good foundation, the best school in the world *cannot begin* in a boy of eight or ten years old what ought to have been welded into his being from the time that he was a baby.

In speaking as strongly as I do in these chapters on the subject of *early* teaching, I am governed throughout by the conviction that on the home training of the little boy depends the entire character of the man. Lost years of children's lives hold opportunities of development, which can never come again.

And if, in these following chapters, I speak dictatorially, it is because in saying what I do, I am speaking out of long experience and from deep conviction. Nevertheless, in thus speaking, I stand in an attitude of apology to some men and women, namely to those parents who have taught me how delightful can be the friendship between schoolmaster and parents, and whose sons have taught me to know what it is to receive boys under one's care, ready for all that is best in the school to which they are sent. To these men and women, who do not need my book, I venture nevertheless to dedicate it.

RELIGIOUS TEACHING.

THERE are two remarks that are very generally
made about a boy's religion: that it must not
be overdone, and that it must not be demon-
strative.

As to the first of these; I have never in my
experience met with a little boy in whom religion was too strongly developed, and I wish
to assert most emphatically that, in the education of a child, religion cannot be too strongly
insisted upon. A little boy cannot be too religious any more than he can be too loving; of
course the religion, like the love, must be of
the best.

Again, a boy's religion ought not to show,
just as his love ought not to show, that horror
of demonstrativeness which, because it is the
fault of the English character, has—as an excuse for that fault—been twisted into a sort
of spurious virtue. This horror of demonstrativeness, though it may possibly have its origin

in the true reticence of strength, becomes too often, in effect, want of pluck ; a reluctance to help others by a disclosure of ourselves and our feeling for them, which is, if analysed, mere selfishness.   The quality of reticence which is born with most Englishmen, and which is so much a part of our natures, is too often raised into a screen behind which we hide our true selves from one another.   The temptation to do this begins very early in children, and is generally helped by their parents because of their fear lest a child should be led to say more than it means, to show more than it feels.   To be able to be reticent at the right time and in the right place is invaluable, but to be reticent when openness would help another, to be reticent when openness is the only way by which we can show our gratitude and our love, is to allow reticence to become selfishness and cowardice.

And it is the same with religion.   Let your child learn that the habit of reserve to God, of reserve in thinking and talking of Him, must not be built up.   See that your child's religion is pure, see that it is *founded on knowledge*, and allow him, urge him, to show it all that he can. You may be very sure that he will not show it too much either to God or to man.

When I say see that your child's religion is founded on knowledge, I mean do not in teaching him try to elude difficulties and explanations. Educate your child to trust God, as indeed he must learn to trust any person who is worthy of trust, blindly; but at the same time do not shirk all the explanation possible; whilst not being afraid of saying that there are many things which all the researches of wise men have not yet made clear. Our religion is what it is to-day, because, in the past, men have not been afraid to face difficulties, to search apparently inexplicable passages and allusions and wrest the meaning from them. Believing in God and in Jesus Christ is not an easy matter, and it is no use pretending to your child that it is. Let him understand that it is because people have not been afraid to ask questions that you can give him answers to so many of his. Let him understand that the Bible is a mine of wealth, in which there is much gold still hidden and still to be searched for.

Knowledge gained in this manner, and from this motive, enriches our faith and deepens our trust. Where all is good, we trust not less when we know more, we rest on what we know when the trials of our faith come. We have not beneath us a sea of unprobed depth, we have our feet firmly planted on rocks of knowledge. We can say, "I know, from this that I have learnt, that God cannot fail in the matters that I do not understand". We need not be impatient if there are mysteries which we are never to grasp in this life, if we are using the faculties which God has given us for clearing up any difficulty which, if not understood, might hinder us in our striving after perfection.

In our earliest efforts with our children, troubles and difficulties must arise unless we undertake their teaching with the knowledge that we are beginning a task which will require all our energy and all our sense. I believe that mothers, generally, have a notion that the beginnings of teaching are a very slight matter; they think, "Well, at any rate, I can make a start, even if I don't know much about it".

With as much reason you might set a man
with no knowledge of gardening, or of the composition of soils, to prepare a bed for your
choicest carnations. The part of your child's
education which falls to you is by far the most
important part.

I believe that the first difficulty which is apt
to face us, in teaching our children to be religious, is the trying to reconcile the spirit of
many of the Old Testament stories with the
spirit of the New Testament teaching. There
is much importance in getting your child to
see that God's dealings with people in the
early part of the Bible could not, of necessity,
but be different to His dealings with ourselves,
for we are a different people, with different
standards of right and wrong, and a different
degree of civilisation and development of conscience. This is but one example of what I
mean when I urge you to make your child learn
intelligently, and it seems a rather obvious piece
of advice ; but, until you have tried it, you will
have no idea how helpful you will find it in
your talks on the Old Testament.

Remember, above all, that a little child can

take in, in the matter of religious knowledge
and the spiritual application of it, far more
than you can have any idea of until you have
proved it. It is natural to a child, born in him,
to want to know and understand about God,
and nothing of deep teaching, if put in simple
words, comes amiss to him.

As to times and methods; it is very
necessary to have a time for religious teaching
every day, and in the morning is best, and I
believe it is of great importance to have a few
words after your boy is in bed at night; quite
a few are enough, and these may be more intimately personal than one's ordinary attitude
in teaching. In teaching your child to be religious, guard carefully against putting religion
before him in such a way that the application
of it may become morbid. All *self-regarding*
religion is morbid. Avoid the "If you are
good you will go to heaven, and if you are
wicked you will go to hell" style of teaching.
You cannot teach your child too early that he
is to be good, primarily, because by so being he
helps, in his little person, the great work of
making the whole world better.

But in the few words at night you should try, gradually and carefully, to make your child feel more personally the presence of God. One great reason for this is that this appreciation of God's presence is such a wonderful safeguard against the thoughts and feelings which are apt, in some cases, to trouble quite young boys in bed.*

In teaching a little child, you should remember that in religion, as in everything else, it is most difficult to make the subject take the part that it ought to take in a boy's life, unless he has been taught early to be interested in it.

Unless a child understands why he goes to church and why he is taught to pray, he cannot be expected later to continue these practices *con amore*. I agree with Mr. Lyttelton, that church-going, in childhood, should not be allowed to become "common". But I do not agree with him when he says, "Let the privilege therefore be restricted, so as not to become

---

* In connection with this, I should most strongly urge upon you the unadvisability of letting a young boy be alone while he is going to sleep. Let other children be sleeping in the same room, or a maid be present until he is asleep.

3

cheap". As he says, little children, as a rule, like going to church. I believe they like it because God's presence is near them there, and they feel it. I can think of no other reason, I want no better one, why nearly all little children quietly and reverently enjoy long services, even unmusical ones. To my mind there is only one way to prevent church-going becoming "common" to a child, and that is by never allowing this early looking-up to God to falter; if once you let this instinctive love for God in your child's heart wither for want of nourishment, you have lost your greatest opportunity. And, like all other instincts, it is only meant as a starting-point: children's instincts will lead them right a little way, but only a very little way; they must be taken early and gently trained into reason, and, through experience, into knowledge if they are to stand in any good stead at all.

Do you foster this early looking-up to God in your little ones? Do you make them understand that they go to church to meet Him, so that they may give Him their little meed of thanks and praise? Does not your boy gradually become bored because the first instinctive feeling of restful delight has not been developed and encouraged, and has therefore passed away ?

Is it such an impossible idea that your baby's heart turns naturally towards the God who made it, while it is pure and fresh from His hands? GOD gives you your child full of the most glorious possibilities of learning to know and love Him in the best possible way, and of showing that love in his life; it is for you, under His guidance, to see that the possibilities become actual. In every child (that is, in every child that we are here taking into account) dwells this germ, and it is the business of parents not to rest content until it is found. No truth is there in the idea that some children are "too dull and stupid for anything". The parent who concurs in this is the parent who is herself too stupid and dull to see the image of God in the heart of her own child. The reason why we have, in this world of ours, so many dull and stupid men, is because in their early years the patience of love that should have striven to find and develop these germs of intelligence, was lacking in those who had their care. Believe yourself to be wanting in penetration, in perseverance, in all that true love can teach of patient care, before you will believe your child to be stupid. Children, especially little children, vary immensely in aptitude, in what we ordinarily call " sharpness," but God sends no child into His world who cannot, with the help of those around him, be shown the road which eventually leads to perfection.*

In teaching your boy to understand the church service do not try to force the whole thing into his mind at once, but take one bit at a time and explain it, and when he comes to that bit in the course of the service, notice the look of pleasure that comes ; he is learning to serve God with his mind as well as with his heart. Do not let your child

---

* I am here avoiding the terrible truth that there are, apparently, such creatures as naturally depraved children, victims to weakness of intellect and of will-power, consequent on the sin of others. This mystery cannot be explained as far as we can see, and must therefore be left alone. In all that I say in these chapters, I ignore the abnormal both in parents and in children.

go to church until he is old enough to begin to understand some of this teaching. By the time he is four years old you will find him quite able to appreciate explanations carefully and simply given.

In the same way with his private prayers, make him understand what he is asking for and why he asks it, and let his prayers be simple. In my opinion the Lord's Prayer should not be taught to children till they are much older than is usually the case. The Lord's Prayer is not a *little* child's prayer. You think it is because it begins "Our Father," but Christ was not teaching little children when He gave that prayer to His disciples. It is, of all the prayers we pray, the one that makes the most demand upon our intelligence, and I would not teach it to a child until he has been in some measure prepared to grasp its meaning. The Lord's Prayer takes up and concentrates in itself the spirit of all the prayers we pray, of all that we can say or wish for, it is the absolute essence of petition and praise, and I think our Lord, in giving this prayer, meant that we should use our best faculties upon it. He gave it to men who had lived with Him, who knew Him, who trusted and loved Him. I am sure that it is not a prayer suited to the dawning intelligence of a little child, though no doubt the sooner a child *can* learn it the better.

If, in regard to your boy's church-going, you begin to do what I advocate, will it be possible that yours should be the kind of house where children learn that the Sunday service is the subject of cheerful gossip at the mid-day meal? Will your boy hear comments, pleasant or otherwise, on the congregation, criticisms on the singing, the preacher, and the costumes of your friends put as the first suitable matters for discussion?

Many who were present at the Jubilee Procession last year, and who were moved beyond words by the manner in which they were taken up and carried along in the great rush and swirl of feeling that was typical of that day—many of those can tell you how they felt when, on going back next day to their friends who had been out of reach of all this and of all that it meant, they were greeted perhaps by the question, " Well, how did the old duchess look?" And if your child has been moved by what he has felt and heard in church : if he has been trying hard to think of God's presence there and to feel some little part of that glory which is His gift to those who seek it, what shall we say of his feeling when he hears the " Well, what happened at church this morning? Who was there? Same old preacher?" and so on—one knows so well the kind of thing.

Can you expect your boy to look below this and see—what may very well be there—an amount of real respect for religion, hidden away under the careless tone, the cheap and foolish criticism, in the same way that one's friend's jarring question hid real love and re-spect for all the noble qualities of the queen?

Do not quite religious people talk in this way? Is it not true that you may have talked seriously and carefully to your boy before going to church, and yet that you allow this kind of gossip afterwards?

Think it over and see how this can be other

than wrong and unwise. Your boy goes to church to praise and pray to God; let nothing happen at home to make him feel that you do not consider this the most important and sacred act of his life.

Do not let your boys have a home-religion and a school-religion. Religion is universal, and the spirit of the teaching your boy gets at school ought to be one with that of the teaching he gets at home. People are apt to feel that when a boy goes to school he has to swallow, with the rest of the school-routine, certain doses of religion; so many chapels, so much scripture; and all this he is to keep in quite a different pocket to the one in which his home-religion is kept. This is wrong, very distinctly wrong, and the mischief which results is this: Boys get to look upon the *practice* of religion, going regularly to chapel, having certain hours for scripture and so on as part of school-routine, to be dropped when school-routine is dropped; the consequence is that acts of worship, attitudes of mind which are sympathetic with the reception of religious knowledge are—in term-time—accepted more or less philosophically along with all the rest ; but, directly the relaxation of holidays begins, these acts, these attitudes of mind become a bore. This is what is certain to happen unless the boy is fortunate enough to combine a truly religious home-life with a truly religious school-life. If a boy has in his home real religious life he will get an amount of good out of his school-life just according to the degree and quality of the religion to be found there ; but you must teach your boy that the *religion* is the same whether he gets it at school or whether he gets it at home ; it may be administered in a different way, but the actual thing is the same.

In any school where religion is given the place which it ought to have, a difficulty is experienced by the authorities about the boy's private prayers. Many boys come to school practically knowing no prayers at all, and never having been taught how to pray ; they kneel down from force of habit and perhaps they say the Lord's Prayer and one or two childish rhymes and then they are done, and the rest of the time they are on their knees is spent in wondering how soon they can decently get off them. To meet this difficulty many schoolmasters, in their own defence, or rather in defence of the religion which they hold to be a necessary part of every child's education, will compile a short form of morning and evening prayer for the boy's private use. Of course if this is to be given to any of the boys it must be given to all; a schoolmaster could not give the *real* reason for its necessity to the boys without making a reflection on the home-teaching of some of them.

You will find therefore that in most good schools there is a " prayer-card " for the boys' use. Do not let your boy think of this as a school matter only, as in any way a mode of expressing himself to God which differs, in spirit, from what he has learnt to say at home. Read these prayers which your boy has given him at school, and if you approve of them, let him use them always. If you have given him a really religious education at home you will find no difficulty in showing him how right this is, because it is to help others that this measure is adopted at school. Remember that, of course, your boy can supplement these prayers with, and add to them, anything that he wishes. A school prayer-card or book is never meant as anything but a *help* to boys who do not know, of themselves, how to pray. If you have unfortunately neglected his prayers yourself, accept this help which school offers, and let your boy benefit by it. If you do not approve of the prayers which your boy is given at school, do not hesitate to say so to the headmaster.

Nothing can get the religion which is offered to a boy at school into the right place in his life unless he has been properly trained at home. Like everything else of which I shall speak later on, unless the home-religion is true, your boy will either reject what he finds at school (reject it in the sense that he will keep it only for school use and as part of the routine, to be dropped with the routine), or he will—if he be a naturally religious boy; happy enough to find himself in a school with a religious tone—learn to put his home on a lower level than that on which he puts his school. In effect, unless religion has been properly taught at home, it cannot be properly learnt at school, without great loss to the home. See that in the school to which you send your boy is to be found a spirit to which you can stretch out the hands which have guided him, and appropriate for him a continuance of the good in which you have nourished him.

I believe that it is in the power of every father and mother to give their children religious education in the highest and best sense of the word. It is not easy; nothing that is of importance is easy of accomplishment. But it is possible. See that you spare no pains in this branch of his education which is worth more than all others put together; and that because it is not a branch of education at all, but "the root of the whole matter".

UNSELFISHNESS.

This is a very wide subject, so wide that it is difficult to narrow it down to the limits of a chapter. It would have been more fitting if I had called the chapter Gratitude; for, in a little child, unselfishness means being grateful.

A child's first instinct is, I believe, to *feel* gratitude to God and man, and his second instinct is, I am sure, not to *show* it. Beyond an occasional "ta" which the baby learns to say, along with "boo" and "mummy" and "dada," one does not expect much of a little child, and the "say ta" spirit penetrates into much later life. Do you ever realise that your child must be taught how to be grateful, just as much as he must be taught how to speak properly and how to do sums? Do you realise that unless he *shows* his gratitude, the power of feeling gratitude will gradually die away until it has to be a very extraordinary effort on your part to please him, which rouses even the spirit to which "say ta" was addressed ?

If you bring up your boy from his earliest infancy to understand that everything he receives or enjoys means an effort made, or something suffered by another person, and that before he should so much as think of taking or enjoying it, he ought to do something to *let that person know* that he sees and appreciates their care—if he understand this, he cannot be otherwise than unselfish.

In his essay on "Altruism," Mr. Lyttelton says, "Can we feel sure that the difference between boys' selfishness and men's is more than skin-deep?" I would say that it is not even skin-deep. A man is selfish because as a boy he was selfish; and a boy is selfish because as a child he was never taught to express his gratitude.

You find a difficulty in your way at the beginning of this teaching, because, in the first instance, you have to insist upon the child's showing gratitude to *yourself*. You cannot bring yourself to teach your child to show you love. A weak kind of pride, which is also apt to influence our dealings with our children at much later stages of their growth, stands in our way. This feeling, which later finds expression in the "If he cannot see what is due to me himself, I will not show him," prevents our doing what is right and best for our children. But is this anything but a foolish selfishness? a bringing into our relationship with our little ones that spirit which is so disastrous in our grown-up friendships? Of course the aspect of our grown-up case need not be the same as that of which I am now speaking; there one must, I suppose, sometimes "stand on one's dignity"; but with our little children is it not ridiculous to let this petty pride influence us? And yet it is this which stands so often in the way of our teaching our children to express their love for us. A child has to be taught to love, aye, even to love its mother, and that teaching has to come *from* its mother.

Put yourself aside, right out of court for a bit. Consider only that you have a little child to deal with, that you are training this little child to show gratitude as the expression of its love to the one person to whom it owes, in the early years of its life, most of the good which comes to it. Unless you can teach your child to love, and, in loving, to show his gratitude to *you*, you will find that he will soon slip into that selfishness which one sees so readily in other people's children.

In teaching your child to love you, as the first person to whom he has reason to show gratitude, you are teaching him how to love, not yourself alone, but every one who shows him kindness, and this is one step towards the great object to be attained, of his learning how to love in the best sense of all, the sense—which cannot come till later—of loving all. Don't be afraid that you will lose your child's love because you insist on having his respect. Don't be afraid of saying : " If I can think and work and make sacrifices for you, do not you owe me something in return ? " You will find, as he grows older, the necessity of saying anything of the sort will cease, your boy will have learnt *how* to love, and you will reap the benefit of love unselfishly shown.

Do we love Christ less because He Himself

has taught us how to love Him? Do we respect Him less because He never fails to insist
upon our showing Him respect? He says to
us : " He that loveth father or mother more than
Me, is not worthy of Me," and need you hesitate
to make your child express his love by showing
his gratitude for the love and care that you
show him, the sacrifices that you make on his
behalf?

I insist upon this word *gratitude* because I
believe that showing gratitude is the one way
in which a little child can unselfishly show its
love. Your little boy puts his arms round your
neck, and his dear soft cheek against yours,
but have you taken care that this is the outward sign of an inward grace?

Do you think that in saying this I am saying
too much? That I am straining after too high an
ideal? There is no such thing as an ideal that
is too high ; a child cannot too soon be trained
to think of others before it thinks of itself.
And in all that I say, I speak with the absolute
conviction that a child's life is brighter and far
happier when it has been so trained. The child
who has learnt cheerfully to give up, where

4

giving up means advantage to another; who
has learnt that nothing is to be taken from
another without some return on his part, of
gratitude shown or of effort made, takes a far
higher pleasure in the small renunciations of
himself, and in the unselfish recognitions of
the kindness shown him, than he can ever take
in the gratification of his wishes alone. Parents
do not appreciate in any way as they should,
that every step upward that a child takes is a
source of joy in itself, and that the greater the
effort the greater the joy, and that no other
pleasure equals it. And these upward steps
may be taken with an accompaniment of complete humility, if the length of the ladder up
which he is climbing be always kept before
the child.

What I do not think you realise is that it is
easier to *yourself* to let your child grow up
selfish than unselfish, ungrateful than grateful, and that to say: "Poor little mite, his
sorrows will begin soon enough," as an excuse
for not checking your child in an act of self-
indulgence, is only another way of saying: "I
can't be bothered or pained. When he is older

he will *have* to be curbed and thwarted, but
mine need not be the hand to do it." And
what is the consequence? At an age when
your boy ought to have learnt to take real
pleasure in seeing others share equally with,
or gain more than himself, at an age when he
ought to be able to feel the love that underlies
and is the mainspring of the restraining hand,
he is sent away to school, ready to take everything he can get in the way of pleasure and self-
gratification; and feeling resentment against
any rule which seems to prevent the indulgence
of this gratification.

Boys go to preparatory schools young enough,
as a rule, to get moulded by the love that,
in all good schools, meets them there; love
founded on experience and a passionate desire
to send out each boy from the school better
than he came into it. But, even if you are fortunate enough to select such a school to which
to send your boy, the school-people are to him a
set of folk, classified as "they": and "they"
won't let him do this, and "they" make him
eat that. Your boy is taught by slow degrees
at school what he ought to have been learning

all his years at home. But do ask yourself whether that teaching can be of anything like the same quality as it would have been if the child had come to school, prepared to love and respect the people whom he finds there, and unwilling to take anything from them without giving at least something of love in return. And, moreover, ask yourself what happens if, perchance, you send your boy to a school where love for children is not the *raison d'être* of its existence. Can you hope or expect that your boy will begin to learn to be unselfish, grateful and loving in an atmosphere where love is not the ruling principle? If the majority of boys who go to school had learnt to *show* gratitude in return for kindnesses or services rendered, a schoolmaster's feelings to boys, and a boy's feelings to schoolmasters would be very different from what they are at present.

Unless a boy has learnt to give up to others cheerfully before he goes to school, he must learn it there by methods which are not the best ones. He learns there to give up, to adapt himself to his neighbours' wishes because, for various reasons, he *must*; he should have learnt to be ready to do so because he *ought*. The amount of give and take necessary in a boys' school ought to come naturally to a boy, because it is not in his nature to take without giving in return. As it is, most boys take as much as they can get, and give as little as they are obliged, and by this principle they hit off a medium, which pleases their neighbours sufficiently to carry them along with others, who are doing the same. You will, I fancy, be inclined to say: "But will not my boy be imposed upon if he goes to school prepared to act in the spirit which you advocate?" To which I would answer that every one must clean their own door-step; if other people walk over it with muddy feet it must be cleaned again. Also that it should be your aim to have *your* boy what *every* boy ought to be. These I believe to be right answers to such a question as this. But also it is a true answer that in a good school, an unselfish boy gets very fair play indeed; you need not be afraid that yours will be the only unselfish lad in the community; there are other parents than yourself who are

striving after the highest for their children,
whose boys are ready, in the world into which
you are launching your boy, to help and
sympathise and encourage. And, moreover,
there are masters and others to appreciate
and carry on your teaching and to lead your
boy further on the road on which you have
started him.

I should like to say one word here about
the attitude of most boys to maid-servants.
I know that this varies very considerably, and
that many boys feel and show consideration
and gentleness to maid-servants, but this is
not the case with *most* boys. It takes a long
time, in the first place, to cure boys of always
alluding to the maid who waits upon them as
"the servant". Nearly all boys do this; they
will not even take the trouble to learn the girls'
names. Of course, if one looks at the question
from one point of view, this attitude of mind
takes its rise from a spirit quite different from
that which I have had in view in writing this
chapter. It would then appear as an outcome
of the faults which I have treated of in a later
chapter, entitled "Chivalry"; but just from this

one idea of gratitude, if your boy had never taken anything in the nature of service from a fellow-creature, be it a maid-servant or any one else, without saying *and meaning* " thank you," he would not allow this attitude towards servants to develop in him, an attitude which leads to much more mischief to his character than I can deal with here.

CLEANLINESS.

IF there are few little boys of eight or ten years of age who have learnt that Godliness is the first great virtue, how few are there who have learnt that cleanliness is the second! And yet the body is the temple of the Holy Ghost.

The impulse of many a little boy is no more to keep his nails, hair and teeth clean than it is his impulse to keep his mind clean. A mind has a much better chance in a clean body than in a dirty one. Of course one knows of many very beautiful and pure minds which have lived in very dirty and ill-kept bodies; but there the mind has triumphed *in spite* of the disadvantages of the body. Dirtiness means laziness, laziness means sloth, and sloth is a fruitful soil for unclean and idle thoughts. Fresh air and clean water are as necessary for the soul as for the body, you cannot separate their health one from the other. I will not say that a boy with a clean body never indulges in unclean thought or act. But I will say that if while a child is young you have trained him in habits of scrupulous cleanliness, you have given him a great help towards keeping his mind clean; and, moreover, you will find this appreciation of bodily cleanliness a great help in talking, when you are guiding your boy to shun anything that may tend to make his mind unclean.

This cleanliness of body means the exercise of discipline and rule which are so useful in accustoming a child to see that a certain amount of trouble is always necessary in the attainment of what is right. I should like to put in a few words here about untidiness, although it belongs but indirectly to the subject of which this chapter treats. Untidiness takes its root in the same soil as does uncleanliness, namely, in moral slackness, but in its expression it goes more into the region of selfishness. Why are nearly all boys tacitly allowed and even expected to be untidy, when *all* untidiness means leaving others to do what we ought to do ourselves? Whenever a boy throws his things about, some one must pick them up; whenever he leaves his books or his toys out, some one must tidy them away. If we are untidy the world must be more uncomfortable for others because of our untidiness, or else some one must make the effort that we will not make ourselves. Let us face the truth that the naturally neat boy, and, very often, the naturally clean boy is not always the nicest boy in the world, is not the boy our hearts turn to most readily, the *boyish* boy. We may still see that the boy who has conquered his inclination to untidiness and to uncleanliness of person is a much finer lad than if he had not done so. We are only saying that neatness and cleanliness are not generally inherent in the typical boyish character, and, I think, if we push the matter further, we may find that this is often because neatness and cleanliness make demands upon the youthful masculine temperament to which it does not choose to respond; it is only a way of saying that unselfishness is not inherent in the typical boyish character. I am not going to say that in the naturally neat and clean boy you may also expect always to find natural unselfishness. Instinctive neatness and cleanliness, especially neatness, are—as I

implied—apt to go with one or two rather un-
boyish and possibly unpleasant characteristics.
But what I want to show is, that if a boy be
trained to unselfishness he may thereby be
trained to neatness and cleanliness from the
best motives.

The ground where certain classes of weeds
grow plentifully is also the ground where—
once these weeds are got under—the best
plants will flourish. A fault overcome is the
opportunity for a better and stronger attempt
at virtue than would have been the case had
the fault originally not been there to be overcome. A little boy's instinct for neatness is
not a virtue, though it is a convenience and
often a comfort; it springs from something in
his character of which it is only one expression.
So it is with your untidy lad, his untidiness is
one expression of his character. Let him learn,
make him see that where he is untidy another
must suffer in counteracting his untidiness;
let him see wherein he is selfish in being untidy, and that by growing unselfish he will
grow tidy.

To turn more directly to this danger of

uncleanliness of mind to which I have alluded
above. I want to insist, more strongly than
upon anything else, that it is the *secrecy* that
surrounds certain parts of the body, and their
functions, that gives them their danger in the
child's thought. Little children, from their
earliest years, are *taught* to think of these
parts of their bodies as mysterious,* and not
only so, but that they are mysterious because
they are unclean. Children have not even a
name for them. If you have to speak to your
child, you allude to them mysteriously and in
a half-whisper as "that little part of you that
we don't speak of" or words to that effect.
Before everything it is important that your
child should have a good working name for
these parts of his body, and for their functions,
and that he should be taught to use and to
hear the names, and that as naturally and
openly as though he or you were speaking
of his hand or his foot.

* The word mystery is too noble a word to be used in
this connection, but I can think of no other. The real and
true mysteries of generation and birth are very different
from the vulgar secretiveness with which custom surrounds
them.

Convention has, for various reasons, made it impossible to speak in this way in public. But you can, at any rate, break through this in the nursery. There, this rule of convention has no advantage and many a serious disadvantage. It is easy to say to a child, the first time he makes an "awkward" remark in public : "Look here, laddie, you may say what you like to me or to daddy, but, for some reason or other, one does not talk about those things" (only say *what* things) "in public". It is bad enough having to say even that ; but, as I say, convention has made it necessary ; and the child takes it quite as naturally as, under existing circumstances, one could hope. Only let your child make the remark in public *before* you speak (never mind the shock to your caller's feelings), don't warn him against doing so. Don't warn him against anything in fact, either at home or when he is going to school. A boy does not need warning when he knows, and a boy cannot know too much at any age, it is only *how* he knows it that matters.

The actual connection between the male and female which produces the young within the womb is a fact which, no doubt, it is difficult to state to children. A very good way to allow this lesson to be healthily learnt is to let your children spend some of their time upon a farm. They will there be in an atmosphere of natural and open ideas on these matters, and will learn things which it is difficult to teach in so many words. And they will learn them healthily if they are with healthy people who make no vulgar secrecy about matters which are a necessity of their trade. But bear in mind that as much of the teaching on this subject as you can do, you should do *yourself.*

The thing you have got to remember is that your boy cannot be kept from this knowledge of the laws of nature, even if it were better that he should be. But I am quite certain that it is not better; the longer he is kept in ignorance, the more time is given him in which to develop that curiosity which is only born in a child, because he feels, within and around him, a world of which he knows nothing, and yet a world in which his instincts tell him, that he is bound up.

It is downright foolish to try to preserve your boy's ignorance at the expense of his innocence, for that is what it comes to. Unless one has been accustomed to deal with numbers of little boys, one can have no idea of the lengths to which they will go, in their search after a knowledge, which, if it be instilled into them by natural and wholesome degrees, need become no more a source of temptation to them than knowledge of any other form of natural history.

There is a fact which is not known to many I think I may say, to most mothers, and that is the fact that many little boys, especially nervous and sensitive boys, practise onanism— "self-abuse" is the usual term for it. This is, if you like, a mystery of mysteries, the why of this being so, but it is none the less a fact; and all the openness and all the cleanliness in the world will not keep the inclination to it away from some boys. Only it is much more easily dealt with if openness and cleanliness have been the boy's surroundings. If your boy loses his colour, gets heavy about the eyes, and gives a quick rather painful frown when he is called upon to concentrate his thought, take this possibility into consideration. Ask the boy straight out whether he does anything after he is in bed to this "little part of his body" (using the name to which you have accustomed him) and see that he answers truthfully. If he has fallen into this habit, make him promise always to go to sleep with his hands clasped, teach him a prayer of a few words asking God to help him, and ask him yourself pretty often, and quite simply and naturally, whether the inclination has left him, ceasing to question him in this way directly you see that he has given up the habit. *Do not* believe any one who tells you that you may, by questioning, "put it into the child's head": there is no danger whatever of this. I believe that if the rule I give in the chapter on religious teaching were attended to, namely, not to let a little boy be alone when he is going to sleep, there would be little danger of this habit growing up.

It is right to point out to your lad in the

first talk on this subject, that if the habit were persisted in, it would affect both his mind and body in a *very serious* manner. I have only to add that I have known this inclination given way to by a boy of five years old, and by many a boy of eight or nine years of age; in one case the child told me that he began the habit before he could remember, and in this case it was a very hard thing to conquer the trouble.

One or two definite rules I should like to add to what I have already said, and these are suggestions to mothers who have so far brought up their children, while they—the mothers— were ignorant of much that, I hope, I may have now made clearer. Don't let your young children "play" alone, always have a grown-up person with them, or, at any rate, "in and out". Don't let them make tents, don't let them play under the table. Though these rules are, I believe, unnecessary, when children have been brought up from early childhood on the assumption that knowledge taken with a pure comprehension contains no poison.

There is nothing but cowardice in shirking the truth, in concurring in the raising of a wall

5

of mystery and secrecy to hide the truths of nature, behind which the devil's game is carried on : that wall which Christ's command of " Suffer little children to come to Me " ought to force us to break down ; for surely the road of purity is the best one by which the children can approach Him.

CHIVALRY.

I BELIEVE that a great part of the deplorable
manner in which young men are ready to
sacrifice their fellow-creatures of the opposite
sex for the gratification of their own desires, or
the possible improvement in their own health, is
due to the way in which boys are brought up
from their earliest childhood to regard girls
and women. Here again the evil one uses
custom as a weapon. He says, "I will have
this sin of selfish lust if possible," and therefore
he has ready for the boy's mind an inclination
which is fostered by every one around him, and
which develops into a general contempt of
women, *quâ* women.

You should teach your boy, and you cannot
begin too early, to be chivalrous. Don't let it
be a method of reproach to say to him for
instance, "You cry at everything, you might as
well be a little girl"; don't let him hear, if you
can help it, girls spoken slightingly of, because

they *are* girls; and, above all, don't let your girls always " take a back seat," while the boys came to the front. It may be good for the girls in one way, but it is bad for them in another, and it is bad in every way for the boys.

Girls are naturally purer and more unselfish than boys, only because for centuries they have been trained and expected to be so, and thus it has become a part of their natures; we do not want the girls to become less pure and unselfish, but we do want the boys to become more so. A girl is trained to give up, a boy is trained to demand.

I have no sympathy whatever with the theory held, I know, by many excellent and thoughtful people, that one can judge a boy and man by the same standard of purity by which one can judge a girl or woman; the very laws of nature prevent, to my mind, such a hypothesis; and it is because it is more difficult, by far, for a man to live a continent life than for a woman, that a boy has so much to struggle against.

This may seem foreign to the subject of little

children, but it is not so really, because what I want to arrive at is that it is a great safe-guard to a man, and a help to him in fight-ing against the species of selfishness which the natural desires of manhood make so difficult to control, if he has been taught from early boy-hood, even from little childhood, to think of girls as in no whit beneath or behind himself.

If you appreciate that this tendency of men to look down upon women as women is, in its origin, a natural instinct, you can then see that the beginnings of this may be profitably dealt with in little boys. I am persuaded that by inculcating true chivalry in small boys most of this tendency may be prevented as they grow older. I do not think that parents have any idea of the manner in which quite small boys— when they get together at school—will often talk about girls and women ; the silly idle joking that will go on amongst them, joking that must lead to worse as time goes on. This is due, in a large measure, to that criminally stupid fashion among so many nurses and servants (and I am afraid sometimes among others who ought to know better) of chaffing little boys and girls about their "sweethearts"; a vulgar touching upon the fringe of real love-making which is most mischievous, and which is productive of a great amount of idle thoughts and idler talk among children. Boys and girls begin naturally and properly to appreciate the difference of sex at a natural and proper age if they are left to themselves; and the little flirtations which follow are perfectly wholesome, and there is nothing in them that calls for this vulgar chaff. But these gigglings, these innuendoes and half-veiled allusions which put silly bashfulness into girls' minds, and unpleasing precocity into boys' minds are most injurious. And it is this—this combined with the contempt which they have learnt to assume towards girls from their nursery days—which leads to the senseless talk among boys that I speak of, and which it takes all a schoolmaster's care and all his sense to check, and, I may add, all his penetration to discover.

In the generality of nurseries, and with the generality of nurses, this idea of the inferiority of girls, because of their sex, is constantly creeping in at every turn of the conversation. There is *no* rationale for the ideas which give rise to this, except that which I have mentioned above, namely, that in tacitly allowing, in childhood, one sex to look down upon another, the foundation is laid of the spirit by which a man gains the advantage, when he is grown up, of being able to despise what he uses for his own selfish purposes. A certain contempt for the other sex has been fostered in his mind ever since his cradle, and lives in him when he is a man, to the destruction of his fellow-creatures. A man may reverence one woman, or even a dozen women, but unless he has been taught to reverence every woman, he will allow the contempt which has been bred in him to come to the front at once when his desires give an excuse for the expression of it.*

For these reasons, put your little girls on an absolutely equal footing, in every respect, with your little boys; give them every advantage

---

* What I mean here is that if, when a man is grown up, he has learnt to see in every woman, the possibility of perfection, he could not, by act of his, help in the degradation of any woman.

that your boys have, and you will find that
their frequent superiority in many ways will
—if properly put before the boys—breed in
them a respect for the girls which they will
never lose, a respect which will stand them in
very good stead hereafter.

Let your boys, of whatever age, associate as
much as possible with girls ; as they grow
older have girls to stay with you in the boys'
holidays, seeing, of course, that they are girls
whom you know to be gentlewomen. Teach
your boys to respect in them what is weak,
and reverence in them what is strong. And you
will find that from this association will grow a
love which, in eventually concentrating itself
upon one woman, will be strong because it is
founded on knowledge, and pure because it is
not degraded, in its expression, by any feeling
of contempt for its object.

GREEDINESS.

I APPROACH this subject in some trepidation because I am rather afraid that before I have finished with it, many mothers will think me so hard-hearted that my remarks will not have the weight with them which, from their undoubted truth, they ought to have. But if, out of all the mothers who, I hope, may read this chapter, only one is convinced that there is truth in what I say, and will act on that conviction, it will not have been written in vain.

In my opinion, all that Mr. Lyttelton says on the subject of "Food" is excellent, except on one point, which I will speak of later. But— my usual complaint—he does not say what he says, plainly or strongly enough. For instance, Mr. Lyttelton says, in speaking of greediness, "Some of the mischief is done at home". I would say, "All the mischief is begun at home". Greediness is never learnt at school, though both gluttony and greediness may be practised.

I distinguish between greediness and gluttony thus : greediness is the taking for oneself the food that one desires at the expense of another ; gluttony is eating grossly of whatever is put before one, unless it is what one dislikes. A gluttonous boy is, as a rule, a boy with a big appetite ; a greedy boy may very often be a dainty boy with a very small appetite.

The first and foremost rule for you, in dealing with your children in this matter, is this : Always make your child eat what is put before him (*it is your part to see that what is put before the child is wholesome and well cooked and served*); there is almost no exception to this rule. There is no truth whatever in the idea that a child knows by instinct what is good for it ; all that has been bred out of our natures long ago. A child knows what pleases his palate, but he does not know the least in the world what is good for his stomach, and a child's whole being will revolt against a certain article of diet, because from its appearance he imagines its taste, and the imagination is so strong that his gorge (literally) rises against it.

Most children like meat because it is sweet (though in a different way to what is usually called "sweet food"), and also because they soon find out by instinct that meat is stimulating. Now my experience leads me to say, very emphatically, that meat should only be given to children in small quantities, and should be mixed, either in cooking or while eating, with plenty of vegetables; also it should be seen that the meat is well cooked; a child should not be allowed to learn to like his meat at all raw. Almost every one, especially boys and men, eats too much meat. Men instinctively eat more meat than women, for the same reason that they drink more alcohol; namely, because meat, and—in a less direct form—wine, spirits and beer, are stimulants to the animal part of human nature. Let your children take meat sparingly.

Children like potatoes, which are not particularly good for them, and they dislike green food of all sorts, which is the very best thing they can eat; and there are many other like examples. But the point of all that I want to urge most strongly upon you is that a child should be taught, before he is taught anything else on the subject, that *your* opinion of what he is to eat is the conclusive one. If he likes what is before him, so much the better, it only shows that he is indulging in a legitimate pleasure. If he does not like it, so much the better again, and far better, for it gives him the opportunity of conquering his own inclinations for the sake of obedience to one he loves, doing cheerfully what he does not like.

But all children cannot be fed alike, you say; granted, but all children can be made to eat what is good for them; and in the case of a child with a weak digestion the above rule is every bit as applicable as it is to the ordinary child. If you have taught your child to eat what he is told cheerfully, you will find that the difficulty of making a child eat when he is ill, which is such a misery to him and to yourself, entirely disappears; the child takes his rice-milk and his medicine, nice or nasty, cheerfully, because he has learnt to obey, for the reason that obedience is his service.

Nearly all children who arrive at a right and reasonable way of regarding food go through two or three agonising experiences— the occasions on which your little boy stands beside you, with a cold plate on which is, perhaps, a half-cold bit of fat and a small helping of cold cabbage. And oh! the feeling of misery and injustice that swells his heart, and the feeling of sickness that afflicts his stomach, as the child gulps and forces down the unpleasant morsels. But once or twice of this is enough; the next time, or the next time but one, he takes good care to eat his fat while it and the gravy are hot; he learns to eat his "green stuff" with his meat; and after a little time you say, "You are getting quite a good little chap about your fat and cabbage," and he answers (with a sort of feeling as if he were scoring somewhere), "Oh, but I like it now," and then is your opportunity for the small sermon which proves that you were not unjust in teaching him to conquer himself, and at the same time to learn to like what is wholesome and good.

If your child has once learnt this lesson, "It

does not matter what you like, it only matters that you should eat cheerfully what is given you to eat, whether you like it or not," you need have no qualms of conscience in giving him a treat in the way of nice things to eat. If your little lad can deny himself cheerfully, when occasion and unselfishness demand, he may safely be allowed to indulge innocently in the "pleasures of the table" when he gets the chance. I know that you will find that here, too, he can put a limit, and that you will see no frown or injured expression if you have occasion to say : " I wouldn't eat the jam, old man, since you have had toothache ".

And this brings me to the point where I do not agree with Mr. Lyttelton. I do not think that it is any use pretending to children that nice things are not nice, and therefore a pleasure to eat; and so I cannot see the objection to withholding a dainty as a punishment. Greediness is self-indulgence, as is the exhibition of temper, and the expression of many other natural desires which are allowed to get the better of us. Teach your child early to learn self-control in this particular of the gratification of his appetite, and the lesson will be all the help in the world to him as he passes on to the exercise of self-control in other matters, in fact I am inclined to think it lies at the root of it all.

THERE are many virtues which you must teach your child to acquire, but the greatest of these, oh, the greatest by far, is self-control. Perhaps the most difficult, and, alas, the most unsuccessfully attempted task which you have hitherto undertaken is teaching your boy to control his temper. You say your child has "a temper" just as you might say he had a club-foot, implying that therefore he cannot walk straight. You forget that this temper is the occasion that God has given him for learning to be strong. For be very sure of this, a child with his temper conquered by himself is a finer lad by far than he would have been without it.

The showing of temper by a boy is nothing but his way of expressing annoyance at not getting what he wants. For this reason, never let a child benefit by showing temper, even if the frustrated wish which gave rise to the annoyance seems, on reflection, to be a fairly reasonable one to grant; in any case he has lost his right to its gratification. This is a rather well-worn piece of advice, but apply it on every occasion that your lad shows temper and you will find that it is by no means worn out. Make your boy conquer his temper himself by the discovery that it is quite useless for him to give way to it.

Do not attempt to reason with or scold your boy, while he is under the influence of temper, either in its first violent stage or in its subsequent stage of injured innocence; you may just as well try to reason with a drunken man. Insist upon the child being quite alone till the fit is over (leave the room yourself if he is too big to be put out without unseemly struggles), and then talk to him. I cannot tell you what to say, God will tell you that if you ask Him. I will tell you, for your encouragement, that I know a little girl of eleven (she is one of my own very dearest friends) who had a perfect fiend of a temper when she was six years old; a temper that, whenever her will was crossed, made her whole face alter, that caused a cloud to come over it, which

6

shut away all gentleness and beauty; and who now is the sweetest, gentlest little lady on God's earth, and who bids fair to be as fine and strong a woman as the one who has brought her up.

Whipping, as punishment for temper, administered after the "attack" is quite over, is sometimes necessary; this is almost the only fault for which whipping should be used as a punishment for little children; but I do think that—very occasionally—it is the one thing to help a child to conquer its temper. I hate to speak of whipping a little child, so I do not wish to dwell on its necessity more than in these few words, and to add this: if you *do* whip your child, take care that you hurt him.

In writing and speaking of temper one is apt to consider first the violent temper, the "getting into a passion" as we say. But, of course, there are other kinds of temper. Temper, after all, is only another word for temperament, and the sulky, what I have heard children call the "stodgy" temper is as hard in its way to subdue as the passionate, vehement temper. But the two belong to different kinds of character, and with what we may call the quiet temper nothing will answer but reasoning. Here, as in the case of the violent temper, the child must be left alone at first, but exhibitions of this kind of temper will last much longer than the other, and it does not " wear itself out " as does the other. To cure this failing, a child has got to subdue *himself*, rather than his desires. It is nearly always an undue sense of our own importance that produces the spirit in us which leads to a sulky obstinate temper, its exhibition nearly always means that we consider ourselves misjudged, wronged. In other words, that we are not being thought well enough of. This kind of conceit runs side by side with a sort of diffidence, which we are apt—quite wrongly—to call humility. This diffidence is really only a fear, a sensitiveness that we are not going to be properly appreciated. The temper that belongs to this temperament is in many ways the hardest to deal with, it is more easily concealed and more easily tolerated than the violent temper ; but it is a source of far more misery to its victim. I would say that to learn humility and to learn unselfishness are the only ways to conquer this temper. It is rather like saying that to learn to be good is the only way to prevent being wicked, and, after all, I think it is quite a true way of putting it.

It is not the very slightest use to think that your lad's temper will be "cured" by his being sent to school. In the first place there is no such thing as "curing" a temper, it has to be conquered. At school a boy discovers at once that he cannot get what he wants by showing temper, any more than he could if he stood on a chair in the middle of the room and demanded it in a loud voice : beyond telling him to get down, no one would pay any attention ; therefore the opportunity for showing his temper does not occur. This applies especially to preparatory schools, where everything is arranged by rule, or by the presence of a master. At home and (in a far lesser degree) at a public school it is different. At home his own importance, and—with the possibility of the gratification of them—the importance of his wishes, come to the front again ; and again the instinctive feeling that something that he wants, or wishes to do, may be gained by the exhibition of temper, tempts him to use his weapon. His brothers and sisters, all the servants, and, more or less, you yourself all flinch before this weapon, and unless, and until your child has begun to learn to control his desires, he cannot learn to combat his temper.

At school the boy is obliged to control his desires. He knows perfectly well that there he *cannot* sit up beyond a certain hour, that he *must* put on his boots before he goes out in the mud, that he cannot go for a ride if he is wanted to make up a side in the school game. He is just a drop in the flowing stream and must go with it. So he is forced by circumstances to control his desires, and so he has no occasion to display his temper.

To put it on the very highest ground of all : until your boy has learnt to say "no" to his desires, you cannot hope that he will ever say "no" to his temper. As I said in the last chapter, in a different way and on a different subject : unless, and until your boy can say, "It does not matter in the least what I *want*, it only matters what I *ought*," his temper will be his master and your despair,

Your little baby who screams and kicks because you try to break him of the silly habit to which his nurse has accustomed him, of always having an india-rubber thing in his mouth, is just beginning to show what will be his great trial later on. Bear his screams if you think it wise for him to learn to do without this disfiguring and unwholesome appendage. Is it not better that he should scream for hours, and wring your heart, than that you should be sowing in him seeds which may grow into that which might prove his destruction? Oh, mother to whom I am writing, never say, "I can't bear it," when, by bearing it, you may be helping one more little soul to strengthen and purify itself in the cleansing fires of self-renunciation and pain.

MANNERS.

I USE the word Manners for want of a better one. It is very inadequate, for a boy or a grown-up person may have a very good "manner" and yet have very bad "manners". Bad manners signify a great deal more than we are inclined to think; they root in want of self-discipline and in moral slackness. Remember this: a boy cannot be taught really good manners at a preparatory school. Sixty boys are sitting together at table; at another table sit the masters and ladies of the family. With all the vigilance and all the good-will based on refinement in the world, masters cannot see what a quarter of the boys are doing at a time. They can make the boys sit fairly straight, not eat and drink with their elbows on the table, or not stretch very far in front of each other in their efforts to supply themselves with food before their neighbours; but unless the masters eat nothing themselves, and unless they are continually "at it," all sorts of minor details, very important in themselves, must escape their notice.

I know that it is very possible that a boy who has learnt to behave fairly well at home at table, may behave badly at school because his good manners are superficial and have not been taught from the right motive. Good manners are of two kinds : the kind which takes its root in unselfishness, and the kind which takes its root in self-discipline. These are the only good manners, that you can trust your boy to carry through life, and into whatever society he finds himself. He will not then be well-mannered because he is expected to be so, but because he wishes to be so. He will base his behaviour on his own standard of what is right and seemly, and not on the average standard of those about him for the time being.

There is no doubt that, when boys get together, what is undisciplined in them comes to the surface. A master at Bradfield, many years ago, commenced a harangue to his class : "Individually, my boys, you are gentlemen :

collectively, you are blackguards". I have
heard it said that boys knock the devil in each
other into play, and I think this is true. The
devil's ways of expressing himself are more
numerous than tongue can tell, and wherever
and in whatever degree he has his hold in a
boy's mind and heart, association with other
boys will bring him out in just the degree
that he is equally present in them. I wish I
could persuade my readers of the existence of
a definite evil spirit, outside their own in-
dividualities, to the same extent that very long
association with boys has forced me to that
conviction. I do not wish to write a theological treatise, but if you could begin your
dealings with your children on the assumption
that there is a distinct evil influence (I always
call it the devil) outside your boy's own
character, which you and he have to combat
together, and in combating which lies his only
chance of allowing God's Spirit full sway, you
would, I know, find the whole matter much
simpler.

In so far as a boy has conquered the influence of the devil over himself, will his actions

proceed from a right understanding of the reasons for these actions. A boy at home may, as I said, behave fairly well "all round" and yet behave shockingly badly at school, because his good behaviour is only assumed where it is required. What I say here does not, I think, apply to the generality of boys. Most boys arrive at school without even this superficiality of good manners to work upon. One may say that boys are divided into three classes in this respect of manners. First our small percentage of really well-taught boys; secondly, a larger class of the boys to which I have just referred; and, thirdly, the main body of boys whose manners are such as to justify what I shall write in the larger part of this chapter.

Nearly all boys go to school, at the age of eight to ten, with very little idea of how to behave at table, and their want of manners is based on selfishness and ignorance. Very nearly all of them will pull out the under bit of bread from the heap on the plate, if, by so doing, they can secure a bit that looks more tempting than the rest; a bit of crust is the chief lure, If there is a popular vegetable on

the table, the dish will be emptied long before
it has worked its way down the line of boys,
for each of whom there ought to have been a
reasonable helping.

Of course these displays of bad manners
mean something much more important than
"the look of things". But the look of
things is a very necessary item in the education of our children, and though what
appears is, of course, the outcome of something far deeper, the appearance in itself is
of great importance. It matters that a child
should not show the whole contents of his
mouth when he is eating, for two reasons;
because it is extremely unpleasant for his
vis-à-vis, and also because it means that the
child has not learnt that to fill his mouth
so full that he cannot dispose of its contents
with his lips closed is the sign that he is not
exerting self-discipline in the process of satisfy-
ing his appetite.

It is a great deal of trouble to teach children
how to eat and drink. It is a usual thing to
see a child—well born and in good circumstances—"smack" his lips ; eat with his mouth

only not wide enough open for his food to drop out; put his mouth down to his cup or glass when he is drinking, instead of lifting them high enough to reach his mouth without his stooping; fidget with the things on the table; talk with his mouth full—where would the list stop? I am not exaggerating at all, although I am quite sure that I shall be accused of doing so. Before you condemn what I say, will you carefully watch the "manners and customs" of the boys and youths of all ages, with whom you are acquainted; and will you see whether *most* of them do not behave as I have described? By constantly and continually aiming at a higher standard of manners than it is possible to attain to in a school, I may perhaps have grown too sensitive and critical on the subject, but I am not inclined to grant even that. I know that in a large family these traits are likely to be more pronounced and more difficult to cure; but remember that, when a boy leaves home, he is going into a family of anything from forty to a hundred boys; and that what has been in your case difficult becomes there impossible. If a

boy gets to school and finds that there he is
expected to behave much better, and quite
differently to what he is at home, he must,
if he has any sympathy with the new refinements to which he is urged, begin to feel a little
contempt for home in this respect. Or, if he
be only bored and galled by the constant pull-
ing up, he will feel resentment at, and dislike
of the new discipline, which is being forced
upon him. In the former case the boy does
learn to behave differently; he naturally ac-
quires a certain amount of refinement at the
cost of a touch of contempt for his home. In
the latter case the lad is just as well-behaved
as he must be to escape punishment; and re-
lapses at home into worse and more slovenly
manners than before.

Good manners mean self-discipline. If you
do not teach them at home, your boy has
forced upon him, by short sharp methods
at school, what ought to have become a part
of his better self, through patient and persever-
ing attention from you at home; and at what
a loss to himself and to you! If your boy goes
straight from home to a public school and sits

among boys who have arrived at some standard of manners themselves, the methods of improvement are shorter and sharper still, until he does reach the required standard, which, be it said, is none too high. If he goes to a school or sits at a table where gross manners are permitted, he grows up to be a man, still in ignorance; and then who is to teach *his* children how to behave?

As boys grow up into young men and mix more freely with ladies at table, the refinements they meet with in their society usually impress them to the length of making them instinctively imitate the ladies while they are present. And no doubt with many young men there is far more than this; one knows, of course, that there are a good percentage of refined and well-mannered gentlemen to be found, but of these, and of their up-bringing, I am not now speaking. I am thinking of the boys and young men whose good manners are assumed to suit the occasion and the company in which they find themselves.

I have hitherto treated this question of manners rather from the superficial point of

view, dwelling, as I said early in the chapter,
upon the look of things. But before I leave
the subject I should like to push in a little
deeper. I have said that a boy or a grown-
up person may have a good manner but bad
"manners," and this, I think, is true enough ;
because a sort of good manner may be acquired, or be natural to one without any exercise of self-control, which is not the case with
good manners. But the good manner of which
I am now thinking cannot be, or become, natural
to a little boy without something at the back of
it, which is of immense importance. I do not
mean now the good manner which expresses
itself in opening the door for a lady, or for a
person older than oneself, taking tea-cups round
and so forth, all the hundred and one little
things which are so lovely to see in some little
children while they raise a smile of contempt
when seen in others. What I wish to speak
of now is what we call "shyness". Mr. Henry
James says that shyness is only another name
for a bad fault, and I think that this is quite true;
he says that we treat shyness as an effect when
it should be treated as a cause. Shyness is

very often but another name for rudeness, a child should be taught that it is rude to turn his face away when a grown-up person takes the trouble to speak to him, that it is rude not to answer when he is spoken to; that, in fact, it is bad manners to be shy, when shyness means that we allow others to take trouble on our behalf without meeting them half-way.

Children are shy, principally because they have not learnt to trust; the shyness which one so easily condones in a little child becomes in the boy "sheepishness," and no one who has not kept a school knows what a barrier this sheepishness is when one is longing to do one's best for boys under one's charge. The shyness which in a little child makes him squeeze his face against his mother's arm and turn a deaf ear to the charmer, charm she never so wisely, in the older boy makes him look on the ground, shuffle his feet, do anything, in short, but look up bravely and seek the love and help that are in the eyes of his questioner.

Shyness is a national English vice, because

shyness means, originally, reticence ; the same characteristic which leads to that selfish shutting up of ourselves of which I have spoken earlier, drawing over our real character a close veil which we put our friends to the trouble of penetrating if they are to find the reality; building up outside this veil, a sort of sham personality which completely misrepresents us.

English people, especially English boys and young men, are proud of this (as they are of many another peculiarity of which they had better be ashamed) only because it is the result of a natural characteristic. Reticence may be a fine thing, it may be one of the finest of an Englishman's qualities, but—like all natural characteristics—it may be made a source of strength or of weakness. When reticence has become shyness it has become our master, we have allowed our character to be dominated by it to such an extent that it forces us into hypocrisy and ill-breeding.

A little English child is generally either shy or precocious, and grown-up people so hate what they call precocity that they are glad

when their children are shy. There is no need
for a child to be either, a little boy may be
quite modest and yet without a trace of shyness. I have said that shyness is due to want
of trust, and if this be so, a child or grown-
up person is right enough to be shy of (to dis-
trust) any one in whom he instinctively feels
that trust would be misplaced. But this is a
very different thing from the shyness which
is so frequently seen in children, which is
fostered by those around them and which
develops into that miserable "sheepishness"
of which I spoke. It is a quality which makes
a child look down instead of looking up, look
in instead of looking out because he *fears;*
he has not learnt to love, he has not learnt
to trust.

When one hears the phrase "a man of the
world" used in reference to any one, one knows
just what it means in the mind of the speaker,
one knows the kind of person who, in using it,
would imply praise, and the kind of person
who, in using it, would imply blame. But
to be called a man of the world might be
synonymous with the highest praise, if the

title had been earned by the fact that a man knew his world, because he had throughout his life looked the world straight in the eyes, having found, through this practice, a road where the hindrance of shyness could not exist, because he has learnt where to trust, and can do it thoroughly.

As to the other kind of good manners to which I have alluded, the doing things for other people, I think there is but one rule in teaching your boy these manners, and it is a golden one : Think of the person you are helping, never think of yourself. This rule carried out will draw and gather into its practice all the little courtesies which make life so pleasant and so gentle, along with all the bigger acts of self-denial which may never be seen by others. The boy who, when he is pushing his mother's bath-chair uphill, holds his breath until the effort is painful, so that she shall not hear his panting and feel that the weight is too much for him, may not be just so ready at the door-handle or the dropped ball of wool as may quite another type of boy ; but when he has—through perhaps much labour on your part and on his—learnt how valuable these little courtesies are, of how much more worth will they be than those "good manners" which have no root, and whose growth is of that mushroom species which may be brushed away by any stress of circumstance.

WASTE.

DIRECTLY your mind jumps to *money.* How am I to teach my boy not to waste money ? By a very simple method ; by teaching him not to waste anything. And the first step to that is to teach him that everything has a use, that the use to which it is put must be either a good one or a bad one, and that we are put into the world to discover the best and highest use for everything that comes under our control, and then to put our possessions to that use.

You ought to get it instilled into your boy, instilled into the very marrow of his bones, that it is of no importance to be rich ; that, on the contrary, it is a drawback. When Christ speaks to us, we most of us think that He is talking a kind of glorified nonsense ; and when He says, " How hardly shall a rich man enter the kingdom of Heaven," and then passes on to say that so hardly can he enter that it amounts to an impossibility for him to do so, we begin to hope that when He said a camel, He did not mean a camel, and when He said the eye of a needle, He did not mean the eye of a needle. But why not? He meant that it is impossible for a rich man to enter the kingdom of Heaven, and it is. If a man has not learnt to despise money in the sense of learning not to value the fact of being rich, if, in fact, he has not learnt not "to put his trust in riches" before he dies, he will have to go somewhere where he does learn it before he goes to live with Christ. And if there is no "somewhere" provided for this purpose he will not go to Christ at all. Knock this into your boy's head as early as possible, just as far as accumulating money is concerned.

But, of course, there is far more than this in it; as I said, teach your lad to waste nothing— most of all, teach him not to waste himself; teach him to have his desires and wishes under control, and you need not fear to trust him with money. A boy has a holiday and wastes it, a boy has a sovereign and wastes it; the same boy has a gift for music, for reading, for

painting, and he wastes it ; and from him that
hath not shall be taken even that which he hath ;
because if we do not use our God-given opportunities, given to us through our possessions,
be they money, time or anything else, the
power of wholesome use goes from us, it becomes inert from want of exercise. And the
opportunities for doing useful and good work
pass from us into the hands of others who
already have more than enough to do ; because
unto him that hath shall be given.

One is apt to say to one's boy, " Do not
waste money or time on yourself," but I think
that one should remember that a boy may
spend a certain amount of money and time on
himself without wasting it. Make it an em-
phatic rule, however, and if possible make him
see the reason for it, that your boy does not
spend his money on "sweets" which he is
going to eat himself. If he gets into that
habit, it is a fatal one, because it puts a
great hindrance in the way of the lessons that
he is learning, of subduing the flesh. The
tendency which leads a boy to spend his money
on sweets is the same tendency which later

will lead him to spend it on drink, and later still to spend it on the unlawful desires of manhood. It is an expenditure of his money for a result which brings an absolutely selfish pleasure, and no child can too early be taught that it is wrong to purchase any indulgence for one's own gratification alone.

While your little boy is still too young to understand altogether why this rule is made, make it and enforce it; he will value the reason later on. But encourage your boy to spend a certain quantity of his time and money on himself, if he is thereby improving his body or his mind. If, with the possession of money, he has also the possession of a heart trained to unselfishness, and a mind trained to self-control, you need not fear as to how he will spend either his money, his time, or himself.

In making the rule about a boy's buying sweets, I may seem to be making a fuss about a rather paltry matter, but this is not so. I should like to write a big book on my opinion of sweets, purveyors of sweets to children, and the reasons why they are administered. Do you ever give your child sweets for any other reason than because it is an easy and cheap way of pleasing him? Look right into your heart and answer that question. You find in your little child a taste which needs no development to make it possible for you to gratify it; he may not care for being read to, he may not care for pictures, or for seeing the lovely tints of the sky and flowers, or for hearing the singing of the birds; all these tastes need trouble on your part to bring out, to educate. But he does care for sweets, and this taste requires no educating and is so easily and cheaply satisfied. Cannot you look a little further into his life and see something ana-' logous to this? In the lad's taste for strong drink? In the man's taste for licence?

I do not say never give your child sweets; what I say is give them very occasionally and with deliberation. Do not let your child get into the way of feeling disappointment every time that he passes a sweet-shop with a grown-up person if he is not taken or sent in to buy some sweets. I think a few sweets are a very useful reward for "something attempted, something done" on the part of a child. He has been using his mind or his body, putting control on himself in trying to please you; and the little luxury is a good change, and gives the little lad a sign of your approval. He will not value the sweets more than the grace of which they are a sign, if he knows the value of your love. It does no harm for a boy to work *for* a prize, if he does not work because of the prize; and it is a very good thing for a child to begin early to *earn* his pleasures.

Of all the silly ways of "showing love" for a child, giving him presents, which he neither deserves nor knows how to value, is the silliest and most wasteful. Of course it is delightful to give a child a present, to see the rapturous look, and the joyous clasp of the article in question. But that pleasure is our own share, so we need not consider it; but do consider what happens if a child is continually given presents until his whole being becomes a demand for them; until the pleasure of receiving presents becomes nothing but the pleasure of possessing them; so that he has lost entirely the power of looking through the gift to the giver. God is very prodigal of His gifts to us, but He gives us nothing that cannot be, if properly used, made into a help to forward His work of ennobling and beautifying the world. If possessions, other than those that can be turned to this use, come into our hands, be very sure that they are not His gifts at all. And can you not let something of this influence your love and guide the spirit of your child to take your presents as something to be shared with others, or something to be appreciated as a token of your love or approbation; lifting the gift into the universal world of Sacrament, where nothing is too trivial to be the outward and visible sign of an inward and spiritual grace ?

TRUTH.

PERFECT truth can be the outcome only of perfect trust, and perfect trust can be the outcome only of perfect love. The more you love, the more you trust, and where you trust perfectly you cannot lie.

If your child lies to you it is because he does not trust you, and whose fault is this? Would he not trust if he loved, and must not a child love what is worthy of love if he has been taught to see and reverence its worth?

There are people to whom we cannot lie. Do you not know some people to lie to whom would seem incongruous to you, while, perhaps, you would not hesitate to disguise the truth to others? Those to whom you cannot lie are those you really love. Our own "grown-up" case is a much more complex one than I wish to deal with here; but, as far as I have spoken, the application belongs to children as much as to grown-up people.

If your boy lies to you, it is not necessarily because he has an insincere character, but probably because he has not yet learnt how to love you ; and, as I said before, who ought to have taught him ? This is especially true of the lies that children tell to evade punishment. If you have made it your care to punish in such a way that the punishment has given no shock to your child's love and respect for you, he will not lie to escape punishment.

In punishment take care that your child understands that you are by punishment re-straining his character ; that you are not punishing so much for the act, as what the act springs from. If a child takes a lump of sugar out of the cupboard, it is not the act of taking the sugar that is wrong ; it is the fact that he loves to gratify his wish more than he cares to obey you. His greediness is stronger than his love. Punish his greediness by taking away his usual helping of jam or cake at tea, and tell him why you do it. Don't say, " How could you do such a naughty thing ? " Say, " How could you be so greedy ? "

The most ordinary cause for lying in a child

is the desire to escape punishment, and the cause which runs that close is that a child lies to help him in getting something he wants or to help him to get his own way. This is easier to deal with. It takes a great deal of hard learning and self-restraint and pure loving on our part to learn to punish properly; it is a lesson every woman ought to have learnt before she presumes to be a mother. But when a child lies to you for the purpose of getting his own way he lies for the same motive as he might have in showing temper for the same purpose; don't trouble about these lies, *as* lies; hammer away at the cause of them.

Teach your boy to control his wishes. Teach him that *no* road is to be traversed to gain an end which is ignoble. A boy never lies to get what he could get by fair means (no boy, at least, that we need now take into consideration); so if you teach your boy to wish only for what is right, you will be teaching him also to speak the truth. If he tells a lie or two while he is learning, never mind, so long as he is gaining on the goal. Distress yourself as much as you will that your boy has not yet learnt to choose the good and avoid the evil; but don't worry yourself over-much about the untruths which are the sign of this, except inasmuch as they *are* the sign of it.

Truth is very beautiful; but—like most beautiful things—it is so involved, so bound up with all beauty that we must not, as we are so apt to do, separate it and try to make it stand alone.

Another reason, much like the one I spoke of last, though more complex, why a child will lie is that he wishes to control his own life; he wishes to be his own master, and does not want any one to come prying into his little domain of thought or feeling. This is generally the reason why grown-up people lie, and this is the failing for which the only cure is true love. Your soul and mind are open where you truly love; you cannot condescend to stratagem where you reverence. And with the boy it is the same. The boy whose instinct is to " manage his own affairs " (it is, at first, but an instinct) will let you in to help him as soon as he has found you worthy of his love.

The truly truthful character is only acquired after much trial and experience; there is no more reason that you should expect your little boy to reverence truth and never tell a lie before he has learnt why he should do so, than that you should expect him to be born with any other virtue ready-made. There is a kind of truth-telling which is easily knocked into some boys, and which is always knocked into them some time or other, unless they are to grow up to be men shunned by other men. This is a kind of truth-telling which a boy learns at school, when he has not had the true foundation laid at home. It is not a bad kind of truth-telling *in itself*, but it is not a particularly good kind of truth-telling *by itself*.

A boy is often told not to tell a lie because "gentlemen don't lie" without being taught why gentlemen or any other men ought not to lie; when to this maxim is added, "Don't tell a lie because gentlemen do not lie *to each other*," it about hits the spirit of the kind of truth-telling that I mean, a very poor substitute for the real thing. This truth-telling has about as much relation to truth as the spirit that makes a man pay his "debts of honour" has to the spirit that makes him pay his bills.

I think that most parents who were asked what, most of all, they wished for in their little child would answer, "Most of all I wish that he should tell the truth". It is very right for him to tell the truth, but it is far more important that your boy's character should become the character which cannot tell a lie. You are apt to begin at the wrong end, you want your boy to walk before he can stand.

Truth that is worthy of the name, like every other virtue, is to be gained only by perseverence in its practice, by downright hard work. Do not value the "virtues" which you find in your little boy's character beyond their worth; do not be disheartened over-much at the "natural faults". A natural fault is as much to be blamed in the child who possesses it as is a natural virtue to be praised, and no more. A natural virtue in your child is a comfort to you and an advantage to him, but it is the acquired virtues that make the character. To be able to do what is right easily may most easily become a drawback.

8

All natural characteristics should be treated as but a beginning, as something to build upon, never as an end.   It is a great advantage to be endowed with a soft heart, a dislike of seeing others suffer, just as it is an advantage to be blessed with good looks or strength of limb, or to be of good and honourable lineage. But the natural dislike of seeing others suffer may degenerate into cowardly avoidance of giving pain where pain is a necessity, just as the possession of good looks may breed conceit, or the advantage of good birth, silly pride and offensive ill-breeding.

Give your boy time to develop, give him all your help and all your encouragement. It is possible for the boy who seems to you to have a natural aptitude for lying, who "embroiders" and exaggerates and puzzles you completely by all this, to become a most sincere man. All the highest virtues mean some fault conquered, some weakness strengthened. Only let us leave no stone unturned, no effort unmade, which may help to develop the best in our boys. I do not ask you to acquiesce in your boy's untruthfulness, to sit down and hope for better things. Very far from it. But get at what this untruthfulness springs from, a strong imagination, a delight at finding that he can "take people in;" a boy's wish to arrange his own affairs, and make the lad see that indulgence in all or any of these means gratifying his own wishes at the expense of others, make him see that to be trusted is the first step in being loved. That, as I said at the beginning of the chapter, where there is true love there cannot be leasing.

OBEDIENCE.

I DO not feel as if a book which is mainly
about boys can be considered complete
without a chapter on obedience; and yet for
any one whose experience of boys has lain
principally in their school life, it is not a
very easy subject to "tackle". I wonder
whether it would sound absurd to say that,
at school, boys are never disobedient; and
yet in one way it is perfectly true, although
in another it is perfectly false. A mother
will so often say, when first bringing her
child to school: "I am afraid you will find
him a very disobedient little boy". One
does not smile superior, although one knows
that the child will not be a disobedient little
boy at school in the sense that his mother
means.

But why does a schoolmaster know that a
boy will be obedient at school though he is
disobedient at home? Of what value is the

obedience into which a boy falls so naturally and so easily at school?

I will answer the first question first. A boy obeys at school for this very simple reason, that he finds his life unbearable if he does not do so, that is to say if he does not obey the spoken order. I do not say that a boy is necessarily any more obedient, in the best sense of obedience, at school than he is at home; but he is obedient just in the sense that when authority says "do this" he does it. In a school, rules are not made for the individual, they are made for the society; the *common* weal must be first considered, the individual case second. Therefore (in so far as rules are concerned) when an individual boy is punished he is often punished for the good of the community more than for his own good. Thus, when a boy breaks a rule at school, he must, primarily, be punished because such and such rules must be kept for the good of the school, the rule itself need not be a necessity to the boy himself, apart from the fact of his being a member of the school.

The reason why a boy will very readily

learn to obey at school, where he would be disobedient at home, is that, at school, it does not enter into the calculations of those in authority that a boy will disobey, and, therefore, he does not do so. No provision is made, no place is there for the disobedient boy. The second question: Of what value is the obedience into which a boy falls readily at school? is rather more difficult to answer. This obedience is at once invaluable and paltry. It is invaluable because to be able to obey unquestioningly is an absolute necessity to every one if they are to be strong. It is paltry when obedience is rendered only where it must be rendered because one's circumstances are such that disobedience to the spoken word brings trouble to ourselves. The obedience which a boy is at once forced into at school is of value just in so far as it meets, in him, with a response from that of which it is but a shadow.

Will you look carefully at this form of obedience? Will you bring to bear upon it the searching light of sympathy and of love, and by that test its value? It is of the same use in the work of forming a boy's character as is the style of obedience, the mould of discipline into which he is crammed after enlisting, of the private soldier. That is to say it is useful to "take off from". Now that is only the first thing to be said, and indeed it is but a small part of the whole, but it answers my purpose thus far, it says that obedience to the spoken word can be enforced without much difficulty. But the ways in which this obedience is rendered, or rather the motives for which it is rendered, may be widely different. A boy obeys the rule that he finds at school because he *must;* if he find himself at a school where love underlies the rule he will, by degrees, obey because he *ought.* Do you want to leave your boy to learn this until he goes to school? Do you want to risk his never learning it at all, as will most certainly happen if—not having learnt it at home—he finds himself at a school where love is not the principle of rule?

Of course in all questions of obedience there come to us all occasions for "blind obedience",

We all have to learn that it is a poor kind of obedience which is rendered only when we ourselves understand why the order is given, see—so to speak—the springs of the machinery. There is only one way of teaching children to avoid the kind of conceit which makes us say, "I cannot obey where I do not understand," and that is by taking care that our love for them is of such a quality that they have learnt to trust us where they cannot understand us.

In speaking of obedience at school hitherto, I have thought mainly of the obedience rendered in presence of the person who demands it; a poor, feeble kind of obedience beside the real obedience of love, and yet it is just this kind of obedience which parents so often find a difficulty in extorting from their children, and which they are so surprised to find is no difficulty at school. For the sort of disobedience of which I speak, I cannot think a cure can be difficult to find. One rule I would give is : *Never* repeat an order ; if you say to your child "Don't tease the dog" and he goes on teasing the dog, punish him at once. It is not difficult to say to your boy,

"If ever you disobey me, I shall do so and so," naming a punishment, and then if he disobeys you, *at once* inflict the punishment. But I confess that I find it difficult to imagine the case of a persistently disobedient child, though I know that such do exist; but I am quite sure that if a child once found that it was more pleasant, more comfortable to obey than to disobey he would take the easier course.

But this seems such a low way of looking at it. It seems to me like advising a medicine for a complaint which ought never to have existed; for children do not disobey where they love. Will you try to look at the matter from this point of view? One hears people say, "So and so has no trouble with children, he is such a good disciplinarian"; does this not mean he is such a good lover? A true disciplinarian must be a true lover, and then all the trouble is made smoother. Of course, children will obey from fear, but that is not true discipline ; the obedience that fear compels is a very poor substitute for the real thing ; the only fear that ought to compel is the fear

of distressing those we love, or the fear that others may suffer by our disobedience; and is this fear anything but another name for love?

I have said that boys obey at school at first, because they must, that means they obey from fear, either of some person or of consequences, generally of consequences. This kind of obedience (as I said of one kind of truth-telling) is not so bad in itself; but poor enough stuff by itself, but it is the first kind a boy learns at school. Through it, if he be fortunate, he may learn to obey as he ought, but this method of learning a most important duty (perhaps *the* most important if he is to be a strong man), the duty of knowing how to obey because he knows how to command himself, is perforce learnt the wrong way round at school, the cart is put before the horse. A boy ought to obey the spoken word because he has learnt to love obedience, because obedience is his service to those he loves and respects, he ought to have reached the letter through the spirit. At school he finds a state of things which forces him into obedience to the letter, and he may, or may not, arrive at the spirit through the letter. If he does learn true obedience at school, having never learnt it at home, it is (as I think I have said of every acquired virtue of which I have spoken) at the expense of much that is valuable in his relations with his home; if he never gets beyond the letter, the obedience of fear, what improvement there is is but superficial and temporary, useful to himself inasmuch as it keeps him out of trouble, but quite useless in the formation of his character.

Now the obedience of home ought to be a very superior thing to the obedience of school. At school an order is given, "Go to bed. Come to me at six o'clock. Football will begin at three." The boy goes to bed; he comes to the master's room at six; the fifteen are ready on the field at three o'clock; and all these orders have two reasons for being carried out promptly, because there are two kinds of boys to deal with : the boys who obey because they respect the reason for obedience, who have learnt to trust the dispenser of rule ; and the boys who obey because they would get into trouble if they did not. Imagine a school made up of the first kind of boys, and then think how differently the orders might be given. This is the kind of school that home ought to be, this is the field where should grow the obedience of love. It is much nicer, much more humane to be able to say "Yes" in answer to your boy's question "Mayn't I just finish the story?" when his bedtime comes; but these indulgences cannot be entertained at school, neither ought they to be entertained at home, unless with the knowledge that the spirit of unquestioning obedience is in the heart of the child, to whom you are, therefore, able to "give a margin".

Perhaps you will think that in speaking of the two kinds of boys who go to compose the school where obedience is a recognised and unbreakable form of discipline, I have left out the obedience that comes from *esprit de corps:* a capital, an excellent form of obedience; and one that belongs, or should belong, to every society. It is a form of obedience always learnt at a good school by the sheer fact that a boy becomes a member of that school, and which, when once learnt, carries a lad through school, college, and subsequently public life with his head high, because only in the clear upper air can one see one's duties clearly. I have not dwelt upon this form of obedience, what one may call the obedience (in the best sense) of boys to each other and to every part of the society in which they find themselves, because it comes into a boy's life inevitably if what I have called the obedience of love has been learnt at home. The obedience belonging to *esprit de corps* lies behind what is best in the two forms of which I have spoken, the obedience to the letter of the law, and the obedience to the spirit of the law; ready to be called forth whenever circumstances demand it.

True obedience is the expression of love. Is there any virtue that is not? Our duty to our children comes always and ever round to the same point. Teach your child to love, and you are teaching him to obey, to tell the truth, to be grateful, to be pure. In saying what I have, I fear lest you may feel that virtue is, in its every expression, too ponderous, too laboured, studied and heavy ; quite beyond the strength of a little child. Are we never to expect to find our little ones spontaneously loving and sweet? Are we never to take comfort in their instinctive graces? Yes, a thousand times, only don't let it stop there. A little child loses none of his spontaneity, rather it is deepened and heightened if he gets the right training in the expansion of what it springs from. There is such a thing as what I may call acquired instinct. It becomes as instinctive to a child, or grown-up person, to do anything when he knows why and how he does it, as it was when he acted blindly. It is perfectly right to act on impulse as soon as we have made sure that the sources of impulse are pure. We speak of a person having " knack ". Knack is the point where labour has made the thing laboured at easy, where the labour suddenly ceases because it has done its work. Impulse ought to be the point where reason ceases because reason has done its work. In the heart and mind of a child should be the power, the possibility of doing right instinctively, because the original instinct, the " blind instinct " has not been left to wither from lack of nourishment, but has been trained through knowledge into the only right and useful kind of instinct, on which we act because **we** know and can trust our impulses.

PUNISHMENT.

How to punish, when to punish and whether to
punish are three very difficult matters to decide.
As I said in the chapter on Truth, these are
lessons which take a great deal of learning on
our part before we can arrive at a true knowledge thereof.   Roughly speaking, I would say
that the more one punishes the greater is one's
confession of weakness in one's dealings with
children.   But this statement needs much
qualification.   God is continually punishing us;
punishing us, in fact, somehow and somewhere
whenever we do wrongly or unwisely; but then
we sin against God a great deal more often
than our children sin against us.   Of course
no one can do wrong without causing suffering to some one, and that ought to be sufficient
punishment, it often is, and it is God's principal way of punishing us.   If you are trying
to bring up your children as you should, you
will find that, when your children do wrong,

the fact that it causes you suffering will be their best punishment. "I must not do so and so, it makes Mother unhappy," is an excellent start, it leads soon to better and higher things, and it lays the foundation of the great truth that on our doing well depends the well-being of others.

There are, of course, various ways of punishing. The way one most ordinarily thinks of is the inflicting of certain penalties for certain "crimes". As to this way, wherever you can, make your punishments *self-acting ;* I mean let a particular and specified punishment follow a particular and specified "crime". If your child be late for meals, let it follow that he goes without his pudding, his jam or his cake. If he come upstairs in muddy boots, let it follow that he stands in the corner. Make your child understand that, if he commits a certain fault, the punishment which you have arranged for that fault follows in due course. Thus the punishment becomes, in a way, self-inflicted. This helps to keep out of the spirit of the punishment any resentment against yourself on the part of your child ; and it also prevents

9

—a *great* advantage—any discussion on the
subject. Of course if, in spite of the punishment, the fault continues, something more
severe must be adopted. But even this can
be carried out in the same spirit.

I know there are, alas, parents who punish
their children as a sort of satisfaction to themselves, because they are "riled," who slap a
child in a fit of irritation, or scold the children out of the room because they are making
a noise. Do not let us take this kind of
punishment into consideration, it is consequent
only on want of self-control on the part of the
parents. We don't unfortunately become fault-
less when we become parents, but I think we
need not discuss the parents who punish as a
relief to their own feelings.   Let us agree then
on the hypothesis that a parent takes his or her
boy into his or her confidence, so to speak, on
this question of punishment ; that he or she
makes the boy understand that so long as he
commits such and such faults, great hindrances
are being put in the way of the work of improvement ; and that therefore he must be punished
until the fault is cured.   Be *very* firm, tell your

boy that he *must* learn to obey, to be tidy, to be punctual and so on. This way of making punishment self-inflicting is practised, as far as possible, in good schools, a returned lesson means so much detention or an "extra drill," so many detentions or extra drills mean a caning. The actual penalties become self-acting, the boy has only himself to blame if he be punished.

I said somewhere that I consider that whipping ought to be used very seldom indeed, and I repeat it. I believe that a particular fault may be stopped by a whipping much quicker, very often, than in any other way; but the main object is not to cure this or that fault which is but the expression of some trait of character, but to get at the root of it. I believe that, as a rule, whipping is a distinctly weak way of punishing, the best disciplinarians do not strike children at all except on the rarest occasions, and then it is done after pointing out to the culprit that every other means has been tried, but that as he has not cured himself with the helps that have been given him, physical pain must be tried. Children, as a rule, despise the person who constantly whips them. I expect this is because the person who resorts to whipping as a regular punishment is at bottom a poor disciplinarian. Never whip your child except as a very last resort. I dislike the idea of whipping children both from the effect that it has upon the child and, still more, from the effect that it has upon the whipper. It is a brutal form of punishment and should only be resorted to as a cure for a fault which roots in some natural characteristic, which belongs to a very old Adam, and faults of this type ought to be taken in hand so early in a child's life that they could not get the hold on him which it needs severe punishment to loosen.

Unfortunately, these faults are those which so often escape notice at home, and are therefore allowed to grow until they take such a hold on a boy's character that when he goes to school summary methods must be used to eject or control them. A mother will say, "I don't know how it is, my boy used never to be punished at home, and he is continually getting into trouble at school". My dear Madam, that is only because you did not, while you had the chance, give your boy that training in the government of his lower self which would by now have made this punishment unnecessary. You have, in fact, left others to do your work for you; and, as I have said before, work which is put off cannot be done later nearly so well as if it had been done at the right time. Into a few years of school life has to be crowded the education of character which should have been begun in the cradle and carried on through childhood and boyhood.

Take for instance two faults, idleness and cruelty, typical "boyish" faults. In many homes boys are allowed to be idle, partly because when a child does not work it is a great deal of trouble to find out whether he *won't* work or whether he *can't* work, partly because of the feeling, which obtains so often, that once a boy gets to school he will be *made* to do this, that and the other.

That is exactly where it is, he will be *made*, but how do you suppose that other people are going to *make* your boy industrious at ten or twelve years old when he has been allowed to be idle for all the years during which he ought to have been taught that idleness is a sin? How else than by severe punishment, far more severe than any true disciplinarian would think it right to inflict except that he must get your boy into shape in a hurry. He must do in a few months, in a few weeks if possible, the work which you were given years to perform. A boy may not have been taught to work at home, but he *must* work at school, that is to say if his master does his duty. But how different would be a boy's first year at school, how much more of advancement would he acquire if he had learnt at home that he must not be idle because idleness is wrong. Unless a boy has learnt to exercise his *will* while he is at his lessons, his will becomes slothful, it sinks into a condition of torpor from which severity alone can rouse it.

Then, again, take cruelty. People say they can't think why boys are so cruel, and they let them go on being cruel, and unless they come later under some particularly good influence, they grow up to be cruel men. The principal reason why boys are cruel is love of power. I would rather say that love of power develops cruelty in a boy unless it is taken *very* early and trained in the right way.

This love of power which is born in almost every boy is about his most valuable characteristic, and can also be the occasion of his worst temptations. It is a quality of the embryo man which can be trained to thoughtful protective love of others, to a longing desire to use this superior strength, this power, for the help and protection of the weak; it may be debased to the cruel selfishness the terrible results of which I cannot speak of here. This love of power in a boy gets its first downward start by the way that people have of agreeing that boys are cruel, of, so to speak, expecting them to be cruel. The first expression which this selfishness takes is "bullying". Boys are tacitly allowed to bully in a more or less degree, to tease, in other words to make others suffer for their gratification. A bully at school is nearly always a boy who has in him very fine qualities. His natural love of power has been allowed to degenerate instead of being raised, but if a good schoolmaster can get him early enough to cane his cruelty out of him he may still be a very fine fellow. But the cane is doing what you ought to have done, by love and patience, years before.

You ought never to allow in your boy one touch of that spirit which looks upon the suffering of another as an entertainment for himself. This spirit which we tolerate in our boys is an expression of their strongest characteristic, which, like every other characteristic, has in itself the possibility of being the highest or the lowest according to the way in which it is moulded and trained. The highest virtue has ever as its antithesis the lowest fault, and both the virtue and the fault root in the ground of a common characteristic. So it is with cruelty and kindness. They both have their origin in love of power. The quality of kindness is only worthy of the name when it is the selfless charity which has struggled into existence, the stronger for the battle which has shaken the love of power free from the love of self.

People often ask me how to cure obstinacy in a child. Obstinacy is a phase of temper, it cannot be cured, the child must be made to conquer it. Get him to acknowledge that he is obstinate and half the battle is fought. Do not set your will against your child's will, win him over to your side and fight the evil thing together. Of the many sad sights in this sad world, one of the saddest is to see a person lose his temper with an obstinate child. It is not nearly such a difficult task as many think to get a child to acknowledge that he is obstinate, an obstinate temper is generally a bad weed in a good soil, the weed must be rooted out. If your child will not when he can, get him to see that he has in him a contrary spirit which sets itself up directly his better self wishes to do anything. This is not the same spirit which sets itself up when a boy wants to do a *difficult* thing, this is the spirit of laziness. Obstinacy nearly always rears its head when the thing to be accomplished is easy; it is the spirit which says "I won't" to the spirit which says "You can". Get your lad to see that he must say "You can" to himself with ever-increasing vehemence until the "I won't" is annihilated. I am certain that you will find your boy answer this demand. Of course it will not be a quick and easy matter, but, as I am never tired of saying, nothing is easy that is worth doing. This, too, tell your boy, and tell him that while he is fighting his battle you must do your share by punishing him when the obstinate fit comes. The best punishment in the world for this (a very favourite mode of punishment with me) is to make a child stand in the corner until he acknowledges that he could have done the thing if he had wished. Get him to say this and you have made a great advance.

In all that I have said, I am assuming that one treats the child one is punishing as though you and he were working together. Of course there are extreme cases when one must—so to speak—withdraw oneself, when one must, and ought to, show displeasure. But this ought not to be confounded with the *reason* for punishing.

The fact that you are displeased ought to be the punishment, it ought not to be that you punish because you are displeased. Your boy will not make an effort to please you, an effort

sufficiently strong to counteract this fault
which you have been striving to help him to
cure; you know that he can cure it, you are
determined that he shall; if he will not try,
he is not worthy of your help, he is not worthy
of your love, he must, for a while, do without
the expression of either. Your help and your
love are what your lad has learnt to value most
on earth, the deprivation of them is therefore
his greatest punishment. Is not this the way
God punishes us? Is not this what is meant
when the psalms say so often and in so many
ways that God turns His face from us when
He is displeased with us? Make your love,
make your help such that your boy depends
on both to so great an extent that, as I said,
withdrawal of them is a real punishment.

This form of chastisement is indeed a
different one from what I may call those *acts*
of punishment to which I at first referred;
these should only be the expressions of the
general work of discipline in the business of
building up your boy's character, the stones
which go to the formation of the edifice of
strength. And may I pursue the simile by

saying that the serious and sympathetic talks that you have with your boys should be the mortar that binds these stones into their places ? A boy will very soon, if he is judiciously led to it, take an interest in the development of his character, a healthy interest I mean. You may talk with your boy on the subject of his own character much as you would talk if·you were discussing a third person ; there is no reason why he should, if you talk wisely, get in the least morbid about himself. Indeed, this abstract way of looking at all personal matters (regarding ourselves and those we are talking to as just a small part of one great whole) is most helpful and most useful in getting a true view of the whole matter of self-discipline. It is the only way to prevent our faults or our virtues from taking their wrong value in our eyes. Your task will be much easier with your boy if you can once get him to see that you are punishing him for his faults, because his faults are the expression of his character, and that as his character improves so will his chance of doing good and helping others be strengthened.

As a general thing, a child has to be punished for acts which, in themselves, can hardly be called faults at all: especially is this true of boys at school, and this is why so often children think that they are unjustly punished. For instance, it may not be wrong for a boy to smoke, not in the least wrong *in itself*; but get him to see that it is wrong to break rules, because rules must be made in a society which very probably need not be made for some particular individual in that society; that, in a society, a rule for one must be a rule for all, and he will then see why he must be punished if he should smoke. A family with one or two children may not need anything like the amount of rules that a family with six or eight children would need. A family with six or eight children may not need anything like the amount of rules which a school of sixty boys needs. But if your boy has learnt the *meaning* of punishment, he will not resent the keeping of rules when they are necessary. He will then appreciate that a society, like a fortress, is as strong as its weakest place; that rules are made for the weak and not for the strong, and that the strong show the value of their strength by keeping the rules, and thus helping those weaker than themselves to learn the importance of these rules.

I hope very much that in thus setting an ideal before me in writing of all the subjects of which I have treated in these chapters, I have not made my readers think that I am preaching impossibilities, that I am too " high flown". You look at your chubby, curly-headed, mischievous little sinner of a boy, and you love him just as he is and you hardly want him different. But our world of men is made up of what were once just the sort of boys that you love so heartily, and ah ! what is not wrought of selfishness, of greed, of lust, of even wanton cruelty in this world of ours by these men around us ? Our true, strong, and holy men, and, thank God, there are many and many of them, have had many fights and struggles before they got to the point where they are now ; and the fights were so much the harder and the struggles so much the more prolonged inasmuch as they had not in their nurseries and from their mothers' hands those early helps to truth, to strength, and to holiness which their mothers alone could have given them; those helps, the absolute importance of which can only be grasped by looking forward into the very far future of our boys, of keeping before us the knowledge of the heights to which good men may reach, and the knowledge of the depths to which evil men may sink. The hope that our boys may be strong to fight the battle of life, the dread that they may be weak enough to fall beneath its stress, can alone force us to appreciate at its right value the foundation that we may lay when they are little. Do not be afraid of aiming at a very high standard for your boy; do not be discouraged; do not hope for more than gradual, very gradual improvement. Be content to look for the goal, forward into the far distance, knowing that you have on your side, and that your boy has with him, encouraging every effort, doubling every step forward, caring so much more for him than ever you can care, One who said—and who knew that in saying it, He was preaching no impossibility—"Be ye perfect, even as your Father in Heaven is perfect".

MOTHER-LOVE.

CAN there be anything to say upon this over-powering subject which has not been already said? This question comes first to one's mind. And yet, looking round daily, as a school-master must for two-thirds of the year, on the number of boys, big and little, who surround him, one feels that there must be more to be said, if saying be any use; more to be said, and to be said more insistently, and, if possible, in a different way from that in which it has ever yet been said.

My own private opinion is that mother-love might be a much more perfect thing if most mothers did not think that, *because* they are mothers, they must therefore be the most suitable people to look after, understand and bring up their own children. Why will not women realise that people do not marry because they consider that they have arrived at the point where children may be safely entrusted to them? No doubt people ought not to

marry until they have endeavoured with all
their hearts and souls to fit themselves for the
duty of being fathers and mothers. But *does*
this duty enter their calculations when the
idea of marriage and giving in marriage is in
question? We can but sorrowfully shake our
heads. Very well then, having granted this,
why do women think that because children
come to them, they must therefore be perfectly
fit to look after them? Do I not know the
mother who draws herself up and says, "God
would not have sent me the children if He did
not consider me the right person to look after
them"? Dear Madam, God did not send the
children, He gave you the power of bearing
children, you have exercised that power and
the children are here; but does that say that
you are a fit person to look after children?
If a woman were to spend all her time from
the earliest dawning of intelligence in cultivat-
ing gentleness, perseverance, patience, and unselfishness, could any one say that any minute
of the time would have been wasted when she
sets forth on the task of rearing children? And
with what a miserable panoply of untrained

10

faculties for motherhood are many women equipped !

I verily believe that some women think that they are " too good " for the purpose of tending children, that to the humdrum and somewhat stupid woman this office belongs. To such I would say that the importance of every occupation in the world, of every profession pales before the importance of the task of looking after and training the very "least of these My little ones ".

When I say this, I hope that I may not be accused of sympathy with the gentleman who sits at ease in the arm-chair at his club and thinks with complacency of his wife at home in her straight-backed chair with a basket of "darning " beside her ; the kind of man whom one never expects to speak of women without his mentioning their "sphere "; or, indeed, I hope that I may not be thought to be in sympathy with *any* man who does not consider that, in tending her children rightly, a woman is exercising the highest virtues that mankind can possess, that a woman who brings up her children to be (in the highest sense of the word) useful members of society is doing a work compared with which the various occupations in which most men busy themselves are paltry and small.

If once we could realise—men and women alike—that if we were perfect, none of our perfection could be utilised to better purpose than in the tending of our little ones, we should start with a fairer chance of having a right idea of our duties as parents. How many mothers are there, at this present moment, who are too busy finding suitable husbands for their grown-up daughters to look after the needs of the little ones in the schoolroom and the less ones in the nursery! If the nursery and the school-room received their due meed of attention at the mother's hands, would she not feel able to leave the product of them, in the shape of the grown-up daughters, to choose their own husbands?

Mothers are apt to think that they love their children because they are their own; we all of us know women who rather dislike children as a rule, but who make what people so blindly call "devoted." Love is a mothers universal thing, you cannot love your children as you ought unless you love all children, not only *quâ* children, but *quâ* souls, *quâ* embryo workers in the world. The most perfect woman in God's world cannot help having her own children nearer to her heart than those of other people, because the love which every good woman has for all children is reinforced and developed by the instinct of motherhood; an instinct which, like every other instinct, can be trained into a grace or into a deformity. And maternal instinct becomes a deformity when it is allowed so to usurp a woman's heart that universal love can find no place therein. Love is universal, and instinctive affections, those affections which set one apart in our hearts from the rest of those around, are only rightly trained where, because we love one best, we love all better, learning to know better what love is. The love with which your child first regards you is instinctive, see to it that it becomes love worthy of the name. See to it that your love for him is such that he cannot fail to learn that all love has its root in but one place, and that that Place is God.

It is right that your boy should love you better than any one else in the world, for one thing, because he ought to know you better than any one else in the world. A child *wants* to love, above all he wants to love his mother; is he not bone of her bone, and flesh of her flesh? Does your boy love you better at ten years old than he loved you at two, better at twenty than he loved you at ten? Do you love him better? If not, the feeling you have had for each other has never been love, it has been maternal and filial instinct strained and beaten out until it has worn thin and yielded under the strain. The reason why your boy ought to love you better than any one else in the world is *not* because your love for him is better than the love of any one else, but because he finds this love, this universal thing, living in precious bodily shape, the most precious bodily shape in the world for him, because it is his mother's. And so with your love for your boy, do you not love his body? Do you not know every inch of his skin, all the perfections and the little blemishes, is it not all dear to you? It is not wrong to love the outside if only we are making sure that the inside is pure. A beautiful wine is more beautiful in a golden chalice than in an earthenware mug.

A boy's love for his mother is his greatest safeguard through life, if it is love worthy of the name. If a boy or man love his mother not only because she is his mother but because his mother means to him the person whom of all others he most respects, his love for her can keep him straight through all, because his love for her has been trained, by her, to grow through and past her to the love of good. If your love for your child is of this quality, you will take heed that *every* expression of it is careful and deliberate, that every way in which you show it is one which will help him to "be in love with love". How many mothers there are who think that to please their children is a meritorious action! There is no merit in doing anything which is not difficult to do, and is it difficult to please a child? I will not go back again to the "sweets" question, many might say that I have already said too much about it. But at the risk again of being accused of hanging too heavy a weight of seriousness on a light thread, I will put what I may call the "juvenile literature" question on a parallel with it, just as an illustration of what I mean. Those dreadful "comic" papers! I wonder how many mothers know that every good school in the country forbids its scholars to have in their possession any one of six "comic" papers that I could mention, all of which many mothers and more uncles and aunts think very suitable mental pabulum for the young under their care. Why do you who love your boy think it well for him to sit with his nose buried in a paper, the illustrations of which are either hideous or vulgar or both; the jokes in which have no point but more or less obscure allusions to subjects which should be no subject for joke? Our children—owing to their youth and immaturity—have something in common with a certain class of people, undeveloped and ill-educated, who support this style of "literature," and are we to allow this weakness to be fostered upon food provided for the tastes of people with whom we should not think of associating? When boys are ill at school, to many of them the post will bring parcel after parcel of these horrible "comic" papers, and every time one goes into the room one will find a boy poring over one of these, trying perhaps to see the joke of a ballet dancer kicking off the hat of her admirer, and many a boy will prefer a paper of this sort to any other that one can offer him. Can this most unpalatable fact be due to any other reason than that his taste for better things has not been educated? The child (thank goodness!) cannot see any joke at all in most that meets his eye, but he is learning to see more every time he looks at a paper of this kind.

Can a mother not take care that everything she gives her boy is the best and most whole-some of its kind that she can procure, be it food, amusement, literature or companionship? This is the continual opportunity for exer-cising all her best faculties, in this *taking of trouble*, this never-ceasing vigilance over the motives from which she acts in her dealings with her children, this perpetual longing for the best for her children, a longing so intense that even when she errs, as indeed the best among us must often do, the fact that she errs with real love in her heart makes the error easily seen, and makes the humility born of love prevent its recurrence.

Mothers, how good you are, many of you, how gentle, how unselfish, how noble; and yet look round, look at the faults of our boys, at the vices of our men, and say is there not some ground yet unturned? Some work yet untouched by which you might aid in making our world better through the hearts of your little children? So often when I have known a boy, and knowing him well, have missed in him that touch of real love and reverence for his mother with which a boy cannot go far wrong, I remember what a lad (who, whatever might be his faults, had a love for his mother which made his life joy and beauty to her) said once to me: "I cannot think how a boy gets on who hasn't a mother he is extraordinarily fond of". At the time, it struck me as a quaint remark, made as he made it in a meditative voice, pondering over another boy who had been in the room, and who had left his mother ill at home; but when it comes back to me it seems to gather so much of what I have

10*

tried to say here into its meaning. Can you not try to be a mother whose boy sees cause to pity any other boy who has not a mother he is "extraordinarily fond of"?

ABERDEEN UNIVERSITY PRESS.

MESSRS. LONGMANS, GREEN, & CO.'S
CLASSIFIED CATALOGUE
OF
WORKS IN GENERAL LITERATURE.

History, Politics, Polity, Political Memoirs, &c.

Abbott.—A HISTORY OF GREECE. By EVELYN ABBOTT, M.A., LL.D.
Part I.—From the Earliest Times to the Ionian Revolt. Crown 8vo., 10s. 6d.
Part II.—500-445 B.C. Cr. 8vo., 10s. 6d.

Acland and Ransome.—A HANDBOOK IN OUTLINE OF THE POLITICAL HISTORY OF ENGLAND TO 1896. Chronologically Arranged. By the Right Hon. A.H. DYKE ACLAND, and CYRIL RANSOME, M.A. Crown 8vo., 6s.

Amos.—PRIMER OF THE ENGLISH CONSTITUTION AND GOVERNMENT. For the Use of Colleges, Schools, and Private Students. By SHELDON AMOS, M.A. Cr. 8vo., 6s.

ANNUAL REGISTER (THE). A Review of Public Events at Home and Abroad, for the year 1898. 8vo., 18s.
Volumes of the ANNUAL REGISTER for the years 1863-1897 can still be had. 18s. each.

Arnold. — INTRODUCTORY LECTURES ON MODERN HISTORY. By THOMAS ARNOLD, D.D., formerly Head Master of Rugby School. 8vo., 7s. 6d.

Ashbourne.—PITT: SOME CHAPTERS ON HIS LIFE AND TIMES. By the Right Hon EDWARD GIBSON, LORD ASHBOURNE, Lord Chancellor of Ireland. With 11 Portraits. 8vo., 21s.

Baden-Powell.—THE INDIAN VILLAGE COMMUNITY. Examined with Reference to the Physical, Ethnographic, and Historical Conditions of the Provinces; chiefly on the Basis of the Revenue-Settlement Records and District Manuals. By B. H. BADEN-POWELL, M.A., C.I.E. With Map. 8vo., 16s.

Bagwell.—IRELAND UNDER THE TUDORS. By RICHARD BAGWELL, LL.D. (3 vols.) Vols. I. and II. From the first invasion of the Northmen to the year 1578. 8vo., 32s. Vol. III. 1578-1603. 8vo., 18s.

Besant.—THE HISTORY OF LONDON. By Sir WALTER BESANT. With 74 Illustrations. Crown 8vo., 1s. 9d. Or bound as a School Prize Book, 2s. 6d.

Brassey (LORD).—PAPERS AND ADDRESSES.
NAVAL AND MARITIME, 1872-1893. 2 vols. Crown 8vo., 10s.
MERCANTILE MARINE AND NAVIGATION, from 1871-1894. Cr. 8vo., 5s.
IMPERIAL FEDERATION AND COLONISATION FROM 1880-1894. Crown 8vo., 5s.
POLITICAL AND MISCELLANEOUS, 1861-1894. Crown 8vo., 5s.

Bright.—A HISTORY OF ENGLAND. By the Rev. J. FRANCK BRIGHT, D.D.
Period I. MEDIÆVAL MONARCHY: A.D. 449-1485. Crown 8vo., 4s. 6d.
Period II. PERSONAL MONARCHY: 1485-1688. Crown 8vo., 5s.
Period III. CONSTITUTIONAL MONARCHY: 1689-1837. Cr. 8vo., 7s. 6d.
Period IV. THE GROWTH OF DEMOCRACY 1837-1880. Crown 8vo., 6s.

Buckle.—HISTORY OF CIVILISATION IN ENGLAND, FRANCE, SPAIN, AND SCOTLAND. By HENRY THOMAS BUCKLE. 3 vols. Crown 8vo., 24s.

Burke.—A HISTORY OF SPAIN, from the Earliest Times to the Death of Ferdinand the Catholic. By ULICK RALPH BURKE, M.A. Edited, with additional Notes and an Introduction. By MARTIN A. S. HUME. 2 vols. Cr. 8vo., 16s. net.

Chesney.—INDIAN POLITY: a View of the System of Administration in India. By General Sir GEORGE CHESNEY, K.C.B. With Map showing all the Administrative Divisions of British India. 8vo., 21s.

Churchill.—THE RIVER WAR: an Historical Account of the Reconquest of the Soudan. By WINSTON SPENCER CHURCHILL. Edited by Colonel F. RHODES, D.S.O. With 34 Maps, 51 Illustrations from Drawings by ANGUS MCNEILL, also 7 Photogravure Portraits of Generals etc. 2 vols. Medium 8vo., 36s.

Corbett.—DRAKE AND THE TUDOR NAVY, with a History of the Rise of England as a Maritime Power. By JULIAN S. CORBETT. With Portraits,, Illustrations and Maps. 2 vols. Crown 8vo. 16s.

History, Politics, Polity Political Memoirs, &c.—*continued.*

Creighton (M., D.D., Lord Bishop of London).

A HISTORY OF THE PAPACY FROM THE GREAT SCHISM TO THE SACK OF ROME (1378-1527). 6 vols. Cr. 8vo., 6s. each.

QUEEN ELIZABETH. With Portrait. Crown 8vo., 6s.

Curzon.—PERSIA AND THE PERSIAN QUESTION. By the Right Hon. LORD CURZON OF KEDLESTON. With 9 Maps, 96 Illustrations, Appendices, and an Index. 2 vols. 8vo., 42s.

De Tocqueville.—DEMOCRACY IN AMERICA. By ALEXIS DE TOCQUEVILLE. Translated by HENRY REEVE, C.B., D.C.L. 2 vols. Cr. 8vo., 16s.

Dickinson.—THE DEVELOPMENT OF PARLIAMENT DURING THE NINETEENTH CENTURY. By G. LOWES DICKINSON, M.A. 8vo., 7s. 6d.

Froude (JAMES A.).

THE HISTORY OF ENGLAND, from the Fall of Wolsey to the Defeat of the Spanish Armada.
Popular Edition. 12 vols. Crown 8vo., 3s. 6d. each.
'*Silver Library*' *Edition.* 12 vols. Crown 8vo., 3s. 6d. each.

THE DIVORCE OF CATHERINE OF ARAGON. Crown 8vo., 3s. 6d.

THE SPANISH STORY OF THE ARMADA, and other Essays. Crown 8vo., 3s. 6d.

THE ENGLISH IN IRELAND IN THE EIGHTEENTH CENTURY. 3 vols. Crown 8vo., 10s. 6d.

ENGLISH SEAMEN IN THE SIXTEENTH CENTURY. Crown 8vo., 6s.

THE COUNCIL OF TRENT. Cr. 8vo., 3s. 6d.

SHORT STUDIES ON GREAT SUBJECTS. 4 vols. Cr. 8vo., 3s. 6d. each.

CÆSAR: a Sketch. Cr. 8vo., 3s. 6d.

Gardiner (SAMUEL RAWSON, D.C.L., LL.D.).

HISTORY OF ENGLAND, from the Accession of James I. to the Outbreak of the Civil War, 1603-1642. 10 vols. Crown 8vo., 6s. each.

A HISTORY OF THE GREAT CIVIL WAR, 1642-1649. 4 vols. Cr. 8vo., 6s. each.

Gardiner (SAMUEL RAWSON, D.C.L., LL.D.)—*continued.*

A HISTORY OF THE COMMONWEALTH AND THE PROTECTORATE, 1649-1660. Vol. I., 1649-1651. With 14 Maps. 8vo., 21s. Vol. II., 1651-1654. With 7 Maps. 8vo., 21s.

WHAT GUNPOWDER PLOT WAS. With 8 Illustrations. Crown 8vo., 5s.

CROMWELL'S PLACE IN HISTORY. Founded on Six Lectures delivered in the University of Oxford. Crown 8vo., 3s. 6d.

THE STUDENT'S HISTORY OF ENGLAND. With 378 Illustrations. Cr. 8vo., 12s.

Also in Three Volumes, price 4s. each.

Vol. I. B.C. 55-A.D. 1509. 173 Illustrations.

Vol. II. 1509-1689. 96 Illustrations.

Vol. III. 1689-1885. 109 Illustrations.

Greville.—A JOURNAL OF THE REIGNS OF KING GEORGE IV., KING WILLIAM IV., AND QUEEN VICTORIA. By CHARLES C. F. GREVILLE, formerly Clerk of the Council. 8 vols. Crown 8vo., 3s. 6d. each.

HARVARD HISTORICAL STUDIES.

THE SUPPRESSION OF THE AFRICAN SLAVE TRADE TO THE UNITED STATES OF AMERICA, 1638-1870. By W. E. B. Du Bois, Ph.D. 8vo., 7s. 6d.

THE CONTEST OVER THE RATIFICATION OF THE FEDERAL CONSTITUTION IN MASSACHUSETTS. By S. B. HARDING, A.M. 8vo., 6s.

A CRITICAL STUDY OF NULLIFICATION IN SOUTH CAROLINA. By D. F. HOUSTON, A.M. 8vo., 6s.

NOMINATIONS FOR ELECTIVE OFFICE IN THE UNITED STATES. By FREDERICK W. DALLINGER, A.M. 8vo., 7s. 6d.

A BIBLIOGRAPHY OF BRITISH MUNICIPAL HISTORY, including Gilds and Parliamentary Representation. By CHARLES GROSS, Ph.D. 8vo., 12s.

THE LIBERTY AND FREE SOIL PARTIES IN THE NORTH-WEST. By THEODORE C. SMITH, Ph.D. 8vo., 7s. 6d.

THE PROVINCIAL GOVERNOR IN THE ENGLISH COLONIES OF NORTH AMERICA. By EVARTS BOUTELL GREENE. 8vo., 7s. 6d.

⁎⁎ *Other Volumes are in preparation.*

History, Politics, Polity, Political Memoirs, &c.—*continued.*

Hammond.—A WOMAN'S PART IN A REVOLUTION. By Mrs. JOHN HAYS HAMMOND. Crown 8vo., 2s. 6d.

Historic Towns.—Edited by E. A. FREEMAN, D.C.L., and Rev. WILLIAM HUNT, M.A. With Maps and Plans. Crown 8vo., 3s. 6d. each.

Bristol. By Rev. W. Hunt.	London. By Rev. W. J. Loftie.
Carlisle. By Mandell Creighton, D.D.	Oxford. By Rev. C. W. Boase.
Cinque Ports. By Montagu Burrows.	Winchester. By G. W. Kitchin, D.D.
Colchester. By Rev. E. L. Cutts.	York. By Rev. James Raine.
	New York. By Theodore Roosevelt.
Exeter. By E. A. Freeman.	Boston (U.S.). By Henry Cabot Lodge.

Hunter.—A HISTORY OF BRITISH INDIA. By Sir WILLIAM WILSON HUNTER, K.C.S.I., M.A., LL.D.; a Vice-President of the Royal Asiatic Society. In 5 vols. Vol. I.—Introductory to the Overthrow of the English in the Spice Archipelago, 1623. With 4 Maps. 8vo., 18s.

Joyce (P. W., LL.D.).
A SHORT HISTORY OF IRELAND, from the Earliest Times to 1603. Crown 8vo., 10s. 6d.
A CHILD'S HISTORY OF IRELAND, from the Earliest Times to the Death of O'Connell. With specially constructed Map and 160 Illustrations, including Facsimile in full colours of an illuminated page of the Gospel Book of MacDurnan, A.D. 850. Fcp. 8vo., 3s. 6d.

Kaye and Malleson.—HISTORY OF THE INDIAN MUTINY, 1857-1858. By Sir JOHN W. KAYE and Colonel G. B. MALLESON. With Analytical Index and Maps and Plans. 6 vols. Crown 8vo., 3s. 6d. each.

Lang.—THE COMPANIONS OF PICKLE: Being a Sequel to 'Pickle the Spy'. By ANDREW LANG. With 4 Plates. 8vo., 16s.

Lecky (The Rt. Hon. WILLIAM E. H.).
HISTORY OF ENGLAND IN THE EIGHTEENTH CENTURY.
Library Edition. 8 vols. 8vo.
Vols. I. and II., 1700-1760, 36s. Vols. III. and IV., 1760-1784, 36s. Vols. V. and VI., 1784-1793, 36s. Vols. VII. and VIII., 1793-1800, 36s.
Cabinet Edition. ENGLAND. 7 vols. Cr. 8vo., 6s. each. IRELAND. 5 vols. Crown 8vo., 6s. each.

Lecky (The Rt. Hon. WILLIAM E. H.) —*continued.*
HISTORY OF EUROPEAN MORALS FROM AUGUSTUS TO CHARLEMAGNE. 2 vols. Crown 8vo., 12s.
HISTORY OF THE RISE AND INFLUENCE OF THE SPIRIT OF RATIONALISM IN EUROPE. 2 vols. Crown 8vo., 12s.
DEMOCRACY AND LIBERTY.
Library Edition. 2 vols. 8vo., 36s.
Cabinet Edition. 2 vols. Cr. 8vo., 12s.

Lowell.—GOVERNMENTS AND PARTIES IN CONTINENTAL EUROPE. By A. LAWRENCE LOWELL. 2 vols. 8vo., 21s.

Lytton.—THE HISTORY OF LORD LYTTON'S INDIAN ADMINISTRATION, FROM 1876-1880. Compiled from Letters and Official Papers. By Lady BETTY BALFOUR. With Portrait and Map. 8vo., 18s.

Macaulay (LORD).
THE LIFE AND WORKS OF LORD MACAULAY. '*Edinburgh*' Edition. 10 vols. 8vo., 6s. each.

COMPLETE WORKS.
'*Albany*' Edition. With 12 Portraits. 12 vols. Large Crown 8vo., 3s. 6d. each.
Vols. I.-VI. HISTORY OF ENGLAND, FROM THE ACCESSION OF JAMES THE SECOND.
Vols. VII.-X. ESSAYS AND BIOGRAPHIES.
Vol. XI.-XII. SPEECHES, LAYS OF ANCIENT ROME, ETC., AND INDEX.
Library Edition. 8 vols. 8vo., £5 5s.
'*Edinburgh*' Edition. 8 vols. 8vo., 6s. each.
Cabinet Edition. 16 vols. Post 8vo., £4 16s.

HISTORY OF ENGLAND FROM THE ACCESSION OF JAMES THE SECOND.
Popular Edition. 2 vols. Cr. 8vo., 5s.
Student's Edit. 2 vols. Cr. 8vo., 12s.
People's Edition. 4 vols. Cr. 8vo., 16s.
'*Albany*' Edition. With 6 Portraits. 6 vols. Large Crown 8vo., 3s. 6d. each.
Cabinet Edition. 8 vols. Post 8vo., 48s.
'*Edinburgh*' Edition. 4 vols. 8vo., 6s. each.
Library Edition. 5 vols. 8vo., £4

History, Politics, Polity, Political Memoirs, &c.—*continued.*

Macaulay (LORD).—*continued.*

CRITICAL AND HISTORICAL ESSAYS, WITH LAYS OF ANCIENT ROME, etc., in 1 volume.

Popular Edition. Crown 8vo., 2s. 6d.

Authorised Edition. Crown 8vo., 2s. 6d., or gilt edges 3s. 6d.

'*Silver Library*' *Edition.* With Portrait and 4 Illustrations to the 'Lays'. Crown 8vo., 3s. 6d.

CRITICAL AND HISTORICAL ESSAYS.

Student's Edition. 1 vol. Cr. 8vo., 6s.

People's Edition. 2 vols. Cr. 8vo., 8s.

'*Trevelyan*' *Edition.* 2 vols. Crown 8vo., 9s.

Cabinet Edition. 4 vols. Post 8vo., 24s.

'*Edinburgh*' *Edition.* 3 vols. 8vo., 6s. each.

Library Edition. 3 vols. 8vo., 36s.

ESSAYS, which may be had separately, sewed, 6d. each ; cloth, 1s. each

Addison and Walpole.
Croker's Boswell's Johnson.
Hallam's Constitutional History.
Warren Hastings.
The Earl of Chatham (Two Essays).
Frederick the Great.

Ranke and Gladstone.
Milton and Machiavelli.
Lord Byron.
Lord Clive.
Lord Byron, and The Comic Dramatists of the Restoration.

MISCELLANEOUS WRITINGS.

People's Edition. 1 vol. Cr. 8vo., 4s. 6d.

Library Edition. 2 vols. 8vo., 21s.

MISCELLANEOUS WRITINGS, SPEECHES AND POEMS.

Popular Edition. Crown 8vo., 2s. 6d.

Cabinet Edition. 4 vols. Post 8vo., 24s.

SELECTIONS FROM THE WRITINGS OF LORD MACAULAY. Edited, with Occasional Notes, by the Right Hon. Sir G. O. Trevelyan, Bart. Cr. 8vo., 6s.

May.—THE CONSTITUTIONAL HISTORY OF ENGLAND since the Accession of George III. 1760-1870. By Sir THOMAS ERSKINE MAY, K.C.B. (Lord Farnborough). 3 vols. Crown 8vo., 18s.

Merivale (CHARLES, D.D.).

HISTORY OF THE ROMANS UNDER THE EMPIRE. 8 vols. Cr. 8vo., 3s. 6d. each.

THE FALL OF THE ROMAN REPUBLIC: a Short History of the Last Century of the Commonwealth. 12mo., 7s. 6d.

GENERAL HISTORY OF ROME, from the Foundation of the City to the Fall of Augustulus, B.C. 753-A.D. 476. With 5 Maps. Crown 8vo., 7s. 6d.

Montague.—THE ELEMENTS OF ENGLISH CONSTITUTIONAL HISTORY. By F. C. MONTAGUE, M.A. Cr. 8vo., 3s. 6d.

Powell and Trevelyan. — THE PEASANTS' RISING AND THE LOLLARDS : a Collection of Unpublished Documents, forming an Appendix to 'England in the Age of Wycliffe'. Edited by EDGAR POWELL and G. M. TREVELYAN. 8vo., 6s. net.

Ransome.—THE RISE OF CONSTITUTIONAL GOVERNMENT IN ENGLAND. By CYRIL RANSOME, M.A. Crown 8vo., 6s.

Roylance-Kent. — THE ENGLISH RADICALS : an Historical Sketch. By C. B. ROYLANCE-KENT. Cr. 8vo., 7s. 6d.

Seebohm.—THE ENGLISH VILLAGE COMMUNITY Examined in its Relations to the Manorial and Tribal Systems, &c. By FREDERIC SEEBOHM, LL.D. F.S.A. With 13 Maps and Plates. 8vo., 16s.

Sharpe.—LONDON AND THE KINGDOM : a History derived mainly from the Archives at Guildhall in the custody of the Corporation of the City of London. By REGINALD R. SHARPE, D.C.L., Records Clerk in the Office of the Town Clerk of the City of London. 3 vols. 8vo., 10s. 6d. each.

Shaw.—THE CHURCH UNDER THE COMMONWEALTH. By W. A. SHAW. 2 vols. 8vo.

Smith.—CARTHAGE AND THE CARTHAGINIANS. By R. BOSWORTH SMITH, M.A., With Maps, Plans, &c. Cr. 8vo., 3s. 6d.

Statham. — THE HISTORY OF THE CASTLE, TOWN AND PORT OF DOVER. By the Rev. S. P. H. STATHAM. With 4 Plates and 13 Illus. Cr. 8vo., 10s. 6d.

History, Politics, Polity, Political Memoirs, &c.—*continued.*

Stephens.—A HISTORY OF THE FRENCH REVOLUTION. By H. MORSE STEPHENS, 8vo. Vols. I. and II., 18s. each.

Stubbs.—HISTORY OF THE UNIVERSITY OF DUBLIN, from its Foundation to the End of the Eighteenth Century. By J. W. STUBBS. 8vo., 12s. 6d.

Sutherland.—THE HISTORY OF AUSTRALIA AND NEW ZEALAND, from 1606-1890. By ALEXANDER SUTHERLAND, M.A., and GEORGE SUTHERLAND, M.A. Crown 8vo., 2s. 6d.

Taylor.—A STUDENT'S MANUAL OF THE HISTORY OF INDIA. By Colonel MEADOWS TAYLOR, C.S.I., &c. Cr. 8vo., 7s. 6d.

Todd.—PARLIAMENTARY GOVERNMENT IN THE BRITISH COLONIES. By ALPHEUS TODD, LL.D. 8vo., 30s. net.

Trevelyan.—THE AMERICAN REVOLUTION. Part I. 1766-1776. By the Rt. Hon. Sir G. O. TREVELYAN, Bart. 8vo., 16s.

Trevelyan.—ENGLAND IN THE AGE OF WYCLIFFE. By GEORGE MACAULAY TREVELYAN. 8vo., 15s.

Wakeman and Hassall.—ESSAYS INTRODUCTORY TO THE STUDY OF ENGLISH CONSTITUTIONAL HISTORY. Edited by HENRY OFFLEY WAKEMAN, M.A., and ARTHUR HASSALL, M.A. Crown 8vo., 6s.

Walpole.—HISTORY OF ENGLAND FROM THE CONCLUSION OF THE GREAT WAR IN 1815 TO 1858. By Sir SPENCER WALPOLE, K.C.B. 6 vols. Crown 8vo., 6s. each.

Wood-Martin.—PAGAN IRELAND: an Archæological Sketch. A Handbook of Irish Pre-Christian Antiquities. By W. G. WOOD-MARTIN, M.R.I.A. With 512 Illustrations. Crown 8vo., 15s.

Wylie.—HISTORY OF ENGLAND UNDER HENRY IV. By JAMES HAMILTON WYLIE, M.A., one of H.M. Inspectors of Schools. 4 vols. Crown 8vo. Vol. I., 1399-1404, 10s. 6d. Vol. II., 1405-1406, 15s. Vol. III., 1407-1411, 15s. Vol. IV., 1411-1413, 21s.

Biography, Personal Memoirs, &c.

Armstrong.—THE LIFE AND LETTERS OF EDMUND J. ARMSTRONG. Edited by G. F. SAVAGE ARMSTRONG. Fcp. 8vo., 7s. 6d.

Bacon.—THE LETTERS AND LIFE OF FRANCIS BACON, INCLUDING ALL HIS OCCASIONAL WORKS. Edited by JAMES SPEDDING. 7 vols. 8vo., £4 4s.

Bagehot. — BIOGRAPHICAL STUDIES. By WALTER BAGEHOT. Cr. 8vo., 3s. 6d.

Boevey.—'THE PERVERSE WIDOW': being passages from the Life of Catharina, wife of William Boevey, Esq., of Flaxley Abbey, in the County of Gloucester. Compiled by ARTHUR W. CRAWLEY-BOEVEY, M.A. With Portraits. 4to., 42s. net.

Carlyle.—THOMAS CARLYLE: a History of his Life. By JAMES ANTHONY FROUDE. 1795-1835. 2 vols. Crown 8vo., 7s. 1834-1881. 2 vols. Crown 8vo., 7s.

Cellini.—CHISEL, PEN AND POIGNARD; or, Benvenuto Cellini, his Times and his Contemporaries. By the Author of 'The Life of Sir Kenelm Digby,' 'The Life of a Prig,' etc. With 19 Illustrations. Crown 8vo., 5s.

Crozier.—MY INNER LIFE: being a Chapter in Personal Evolution and Autobiography. By JOHN BEATTIE CROZIER, Author of 'Civilization and Progress,' etc. 8vo., 14s.

Dante.—THE LIFE AND WORKS OF DANTE ALLIGHIERI: being an Introduction to the Study of the 'Divina Commedia'. By the Rev. J. F. HOGAN, D.D., Professor, St. Patrick's College, Maynooth. With Portrait. 8vo.

Danton.—LIFE OF DANTON. By A. H. BEESLY. With Portraits of Danton, his Mother, and an Illustration of the Home of his Family at Arcis. Crown 8vo., 6s.

Duncan.—ADMIRAL DUNCAN. By the EARL OF CAMPERDOWN. With 3 Portraits. 8vo., 16s.

Erasmus.—LIFE AND LETTERS OF ERASMUS. By JAMES ANTHONY FROUDE. Crown 8vo., 3s. 6d.

Faraday. — FARADAY AS A DISCOVERER. By JOHN TYNDALL. Cr. 8vo., 3s. 6d.

FOREIGN COURTS AND FOREIGN HOMES. By A. M. F. Crown 8vo., 6s.

Biography, Personal Memoirs, &c.—*continued.*

Fox.—THE EARLY HISTORY OF CHARLES JAMES FOX. By the Right Hon. Sir G. O. TREVELYAN, Bart.
Library Edition. 8vo., 18*s.*
'*Silver Library' Edition.* Crown 8vo., 3*s.* 6*d.*

Halifax.—THE LIFE AND LETTERS OF SIR GEORGE SAVILE, BARONET, FIRST MARQUIS OF HALIFAX. By H. C. FOXCROFT. 2 vols. 8vo., 36*s.*

Hamilton.—LIFE OF SIR WILLIAM HAMILTON. By R. P. GRAVES. 8vo. 3 vols. 15*s.* each. ADDENDUM. 8vo., 6*d.* sewed.

Havelock.—MEMOIRS OF SIR HENRY HAVELOCK, K.C.B. By JOHN CLARK MARSHMAN. Crown 8vo., 3*s.* 6*d.*

Haweis.—MY MUSICAL LIFE. By the Rev. H. R. HAWEIS. With Portrait of Richard Wagner and 3 Illustrations. Crown 8vo., 7*s.* 6*d.*

Hiley.—MEMORIES OF HALF A CENTURY. By the Rev. W. R. HILEY, D.D., Vicar of Wighill, Tadcaster. With Portrait. 8vo., 15*s.*

Jackson.—STONEWALL JACKSON AND THE AMERICAN CIVIL WAR. By Lieut.-Col. G. F. R. HENDERSON. With 2 Portraits and 33 Maps and Plans. 2 vols. 8vo., 42*s.*

Leslie.—THE LIFE AND CAMPAIGNS OF ALEXANDER LESLIE, FIRST EARL OF LEVEN. By CHARLES SANFORD TERRY, M.A. With Maps and Plans. 8vo., 16*s.*

Luther.—LIFE OF LUTHER. By JULIUS KÖSTLIN. With 62 Illustrations and 4 Facsimiles of MSS. Crown 8vo., 3*s.* 6*d.*

Macaulay.—THE LIFE AND LETTERS OF LORD MACAULAY. By the Right Hon. Sir G. O. TREVELYAN, Bart.,
Popular Edit. 1 vol. Cr. 8vo., 2*s.* 6*d.*
Student's Edition. 1 vol. Cr. 8vo., 6*s.*
Cabinet Edition. 2 vols. Post 8vo., 12*s.*
'*Edinburgh Edition.*' 2 vols. 8vo., 6*s.* each.
Library Edition. 2 vols. 8vo., 36*s.*

Marbot.—THE MEMOIRS OF THE BARON DE MARBOT. Translated from the French. 2 vols. Crown 8vo., 7*s.*

Max Müller.—AULD LANG SYNE. By the Right Hon. F. MAX MÜLLER. First Series. With Portrait. 8vo., 10*s.* 6*d.*
Second Series. MY INDIAN FRIENDS. 8vo., 10*s.* 6*d.*

Morris.—THE LIFE OF WILLIAM MORRIS. By J. W. MACKAIL. With 6 Portraits and 16 Illustrations by E. H. NEW. 2 vols. 8vo., 32*s.*

Palgrave.—FRANCIS TURNER PALGRAVE : his Journals, and Memories of his Life. By GWENLLIAN F. PALGRAVE. With Portrait and Illustration. 8vo., 10*s.* 6*d.*

Place.—THE LIFE OF FRANCIS PLACE, 1771-1854. By GRAHAM WALLAS, M.A. With 2 Portraits. 8vo., 12*s.*

Powys.—PASSAGES FROM THE DIARIES OF MRS. PHILIP LYBBE POWYS, of Hardwick House, Oxon., 1756-1808. Edited by EMILY J. CLIMENSON. With 2 Pedigrees (Lybbe and Powys) and Photogravure Portrait. 8vo., 16*s.*

RÂMAKRISHNA : HIS LIFE AND SAYINGS. By the Right Hon. F. MAX MÜLLER. Crown 8vo., 5*s.*

Reeve.—MEMOIRS OF THE LIFE AND CORRESPONDENCE OF HENRY REEVE, C.B., late Editor of the 'Edinburgh Review'. By JOHN KNOX LAUGHTON, M.A. With 2 Portraits. 2 vols. 8vo., 28*s.*

Romanes.—THE LIFE AND LETTERS OF GEORGE JOHN ROMANES, M.A., LL.D., F.R.S. Written and Edited by his Wife. With Portrait and 2 Illustrations. Cr. 8vo., 6*s.*

Seebohm.—THE OXFORD REFORMERS —JOHN COLET, ERASMUS AND THOMAS MORE : a History of their Fellow-Work. By FREDERIC SEEBOHM. 8vo., 14*s.*

Shakespeare.—OUTLINES OF THE LIFE OF SHAKESPEARE. By J. O. HALLIWELL-PHILLIPPS. With Illustrations and Facsimiles. 2 vols. Royal 8vo., 21*s.*

Shakespeare's TRUE LIFE. By JAS. WALTER. With 500 Illustrations by GERALD E. MOIRA. Imp. 8vo., 21*s.*

Stanley (LADY).
THE GIRLHOOD OF MARIA JOSEPHA HOLROYD (Lady Stanley of Alderly). Recorded in Letters of a Hundred Years Ago, from 1776-1796. Edited by J. H. ADEANE. With 6 Portraits. 8vo., 18*s.*

THE EARLY MARRIED LIFE OF MARIA JOSEPHA, LADY STANLEY, FROM 1796. Edited by J. H. ADEANE. With 10 Portraits and 3 Illustrations. 8vo., 18*s.*

Biography, Personal Memoirs, &c.—*continued.*

Turgot.—THE LIFE AND WRITINGS OF TURGOT, Comptroller-General of France, 1774-1776. Edited for English Readers by W. WALKER STEPHENS. With Portrait. 8vo., 7s. 6d.

Verney.—MEMOIRS OF THE VERNEY FAMILY. Compiled from the Letters and Illustrated by the Portraits at Clayden House.

Vols. I. and II. DURING THE CIVIL WAR. By FRANCES PARTHENOPE VERNEY. With 38 Portraits, Woodcuts and Facsimile. Royal 8vo., 42s.

Verney.—MEMOIRS OF THE VERNEY FAMILY—*continued.*

Vol. III. DURING THE COMMONWEALTH. 1650-1660. By MARGARET M. VERNEY. With 10 Portraits, &c. Royal 8vo., 21s.

Vol. IV. FROM THE RESTORATION TO THE REVOLUTION. 1660 to 1696. By MARGARET M. VERNEY. With Portraits. Royal 8vo., 21s.

Wellington.—LIFE OF THE DUKE OF WELLINGTON. By the Rev. G. R. GLEIG, M.A. Crown 8vo., 3s. 6d.

Travel and Adventure, the Colonies, &c.

Arnold.—SEAS AND LANDS. By Sir EDWIN ARNOLD. With 71 Illustrations. Crown 8vo., 3s. 6d.

Baker (Sir S. W.).
EIGHT YEARS IN CEYLON. With 6 Illustrations. Crown 8vo., 3s. 6d.
THE RIFLE AND THE HOUND IN CEYLON. With 6 Illustrations. Cr. 8vo., 3s. 6d.

Ball (JOHN).
THE ALPINE GUIDE. Reconstructed and Revised on behalf of the Alpine Club, by W. A. B. COOLIDGE.
Vol. I. THE WESTERN ALPS; The Alpine Region, South of the Rhone Valley, from the Col de Tenda to the Simplon Pass. With 9 New and Revised Maps. Crown 8vo., 12s. net.
HINTS AND NOTES, PRACTICAL AND SCIENTIFIC, FOR TRAVELLERS IN THE ALPS : being a Revision of the General Introduction to the 'Alpine Guide'. Crown 8vo., 3s. net.

Bent.—THE RUINED CITIES OF MASHONALAND : being a Record of Excavation and Exploration in 1891. By J. THEODORE BENT. With 117 Illustrations. Crown 8vo., 3s. 6d.

Bicknell.—TRAVEL AND ADVENTURE IN NORTHERN QUEENSLAND. By ARTHUR C. BICKNELL. With 24 Plates and 22 Illustrations in the Text. 8vo., 15s.

Brassey.—VOYAGES AND TRAVELS OF LORD BRASSEY, K.C.B., D.C.L., 1862-1894. Arranged and Edited by Captain S. EARDLEY-WILMOT. 2 vols. Cr. 8vo., 10s.

Brassey (The late LADY).
A VOYAGE IN THE 'SUNBEAM'; OUR HOME ON THE OCEAN FOR ELEVEN MONTHS.
Cabinet Edition. With Map and 66 Illustrations. Crown 8vo., 7s. 6d.
'*Silver Library*' *Edition.* With 66 Illustrations. Crown 8vo., 3s. 6d.
Popular Edition. With 60 Illustrations. 4to., 6d. sewed, 1s. cloth.
School Edition. With 37 Illustrations. Fcp., 2s. cloth, or 3s. white parchment.
SUNSHINE AND STORM IN THE EAST.
Cabinet Edition. With 2 Maps and 114 Illustrations. Crown 8vo., 7s. 6d.
Popular Edition. With 103 Illustrations. 4to., 6d. sewed, 1s. cloth.
IN THE TRADES, THE TROPICS, AND THE ' ROARING FORTIES'.
Cabinet Edition. With Map and 220 Illustrations. Crown 8vo., 7s. 6d.

Browning.—A GIRL'S WANDERINGS IN HUNGARY. By H. ELLEN BROWNING. With Map and 20 Illustrations. Crown 8vo., 3s. 6d.

Churchill. — THE STORY OF THE MALAKAND FIELD FORCE, 1897. By WINSTON SPENCER CHURCHILL. With 6 Maps and Plans. Cr. 8vo., 3s. 6d.

Froude (JAMES A.).
OCEANA : or England and her Colonies. With 9 Illustrations. Crown 8vo., 3s. 6d.
THE ENGLISH IN THE WEST INDIES : or, the Bow of Ulysses. With 9 Illustrations. Cr. 8vo., 2s. bds., 2s. 6d. cl.

Travel and Adventure, the Colonies, &c.—*continued.*

Howitt.—Visits to Remarkable Places, Old Halls, Battle-Fields, Scenes, illustrative of Striking Passages in English History and Poetry. By William Howitt. With 80 Illustrations. Crown 8vo., 3*s.* 6*d.*

Knight (E. F.).

THE CRUISE OF THE 'ALERTE': the Narrative of a Search for Treasure on the Desert Island of Trinidad. With 2 Maps and 23 Illustrations. Crown 8vo., 3*s.* 6*d.*

WHERE THREE EMPIRES MEET: a Narrative of Recent Travel in Kashmir, Western Tibet, Baltistan, Ladak, Gilgit, and the adjoining Countries. With a Map and 54 Illustrations. Cr. 8vo., 3*s.* 6*d.*

THE 'FALCON' ON THE BALTIC: a Voyage from London to Copenhagen in a Three-Tonner. With 10 Full-page Illustrations. Cr. 8vo., 3*s.* 6*d.*

Lees.—PEAKS AND PINES: another Norway Book. By J. A. LEES. With 63 Illustrations and Photographs Cr, 8vo., 6*s.*

Lees and Clutterbuck.—B. C. 1887: A RAMBLE IN BRITISH COLUMBIA. By J. A. LEES and W. J. CLUTTERBUCK. With Map and 75 Illustrations. Cr. 8vo., 3*s.* 6*d.*

Macdonald. — THE GOLD COAST: PAST AND PRESENT. By GEORGE MACDONALD. With 32 Illustrations. Crown 8vo., 7*s.* 6*d.*

Nansen. — THE FIRST CROSSING OF GREENLAND. By FRIDTJOF NANSEN. With 143 Illustrations and a Map. Cr. 8vo., 3*s.* 6*d.*

Phillips. — SOUTH AFRICAN RECOLLECTIONS. By FLORENCE PHILLIPS (Mrs. LIONEL PHILLIPS). With 37 Illustrations. 8vo., 7*s.* 6*d.*

Smith.—CLIMBING IN THE BRITISH ISLES. By W. P. HASKETT SMITH. With Illustrations by ELLIS CARR, and Numerous Plans.
Part I. ENGLAND. 16mo., 3*s.* 6*d.*
Part II. WALES AND IRELAND. 16mo., 3*s.* 6*d.*

Stephen. — THE PLAYGROUND OF EUROPE (The Alps). By LESLIE STEPHEN. With 4 Illustrations. Crown 8vo., 3*s.* 6*d.*

THREE IN NORWAY. By Two of Them. With a Map and 59 Illustrations. Cr. 8vo., 2*s.* boards, 2*s.* 6*d.* cloth.

Tyndall (JOHN).

THE GLACIERS OF THE ALPS: being a Narrative of Excursions and Ascents. An Account of the Origin and Phenomena of Glaciers, and an Exposition of the Physical Principles to which they are related. With 61 Illustrations. Crown 8vo., 6*s.* 6*d.* net.

HOURS OF EXERCISE IN THE ALPS. With 7 Illustrations. Cr. 8vo., 6*s.* 6*d.* net.

Vivian.—SERVIA: the Poor Man's Paradise. By HERBERT VIVIAN, M.A., Officer of the Royal Order of Takovo. With Map and Portrait of King Alexander. 8vo., 15*s.*

Sport and Pastime.
THE BADMINTON LIBRARY.
Edited by HIS GRACE THE DUKE OF BEAUFORT, K.G., and A. E. T. WATSON.
Complete in 28 Volumes. Crown 8vo., Price 10*s.* 6*d.* each Volume, Cloth.

** *The Volumes are also issued half-bound in Leather, with gilt top. The price can be had from all Booksellers.*

ARCHERY. By C. J. LONGMAN and Col. H. WALROND. With Contributions by Miss LEGH, Viscount DILLON, &c. With 2 Maps, 23 Plates, and 172 Illustrations in the Text. Crown 8vo., 10*s.* 6*d.*

ATHLETICS. By MONTAGUE SHEARMAN. With Chapters on Athletics at School by W. BEACHER THOMAS; Athletic Sports in America by C. H. SHERRILL; a Contribution on Paper-chasing by W. RYE, and an Introduction by Sir RICHARD WEBSTER, Q.C., M.P. With 12 Plates and 37 Illustrations in the Text. Crown 8vo., 10*s.* 6*d.*

Sport and Pastime—*continued.*

THE BADMINTON LIBRARY—*continued.*

BIG GAME SHOOTING. By CLIVE PHILLIPPS-WOLLEY.

Vol. I. AFRICA AND AMERICA. With Contributions by Sir SAMURL W. BAKER, W. C. OSWELL, F. C. SELOUS, &c. With 20 Plates and 57 Illustrations in the Text. Crown 8vo., 10s. 6d.

Vol. II. EUROPE, ASIA, AND THE ARCTIC REGIONS. With Contributions by Lieut.-Colonel R. HEBER PERCY, Major ALGERNON C. HEBER PERCY, &c. With 17 Plates and 56 Illustrations in the Text. Crown 8vo., 10s. 6d.

BILLIARDS. By Major W. BROADFOOT, R.E. With Contributions by A. H. BOYD, SYDENHAM DIXON, W. J. FORD, &c. With 11 Plates, 19 Illustrations in the Text, and numerous Diagrams. Crown 8vo., 10s. 6d.

COURSING AND FALCONRY. By HARDING COX, CHARLES RICHARDSON, and the Hon. GERALD LASCELLES. With 20 Plates and 55 Illustrations in the Text. Crown 8vo., 10s. 6d.

CRICKET. By A. G. STEEL, and the Hon. R. H. LYTTELTON. With Contributions by ANDREW LANG, W. G. GRACE, F. GALE, &c. With 13 Plates and 52 Illustrations in the Text. Crown 8vo., 10s. 6d.

CYCLING. By the EARL OF ALBEMARLE, and G. LACY HILLIER. With 19 Plates and 44 Illustrations in the Text. Crown 8vo., 10s. 6d.

DANCING. By Mrs. LILLY GROVE, F.R.G.S. With Contributions by Miss MIDDLETON, The Hon. Mrs. ARMYTAGE, &c. With Musical Examples, and 38 Full-page Plates and 93 Illustrations in the Text. Cr. 8vo., 10s. 6d.

DRIVING. By His Grace the DUKE OF BEAUFORT, K.G. With Contributions by A. E. T. WATSON. the EARL OF ONSLOW, &c. With 12 Plates and 54 Illustrations in the Text. Crown 8vo., 10s. 6d.

FENCING, BOXING, AND WRESTLING. By WALTER H. POLLOCK, F. C. GROVE, C. PREVOST, E. B. MITCHELL, and WALTER ARMSTRONG. With 18 Plates and 24 Illustrations in the Text. Crown 8vo., 10s. 6d.

FISHING. By H. CHOLMONDELEY-PENNELL.

Vol. I. SALMON AND TROUT. With Contributions by H. R. FRANCIS, Major JOHN P. TRAHERNE, &c. With 9 Plates and numerous Illustrations of Tackle, &c. Crown 8vo., 10s. 6d.

Vol. II. PIKE AND OTHER COARSE FISH. With Contributions by the MARQUIS OF EXETER, WILLIAM SENIOR, G. CHRISTOPHER DAVIS, &c. With 7 Plates and numerous Illustrations of Tackle, &c. Crown 8vo., 10s. 6d.

FOOTBALL. By MONTAGUE SHEARMAN, W. J. OAKLEY, G. O. SMITH, FRANK MITCHELL, &c. With 19 Plates and 35 Illustrations in the Text. Cr. 8vo., 10s. 6d.

GOLF. By HORACE G. HUTCHINSON. With Contributions by the Rt. Hon. A. J. BALFOUR, M.P., Sir WALTER SIMPSON, Bart., ANDREW LANG, &c. With 32 Plates and 57 Illustrations in the Text. Cr. 8vo., 10s. 6d.

HUNTING. By His Grace the DUKE OF BEAUFORT K.G., and MOWBRAY MORRIS. With Contributions by the EARL OF SUFFOLK AND BERKSHIRE, Rev. E. W. L. DAVIES, G. H. LONGMAN, &c. With 5 Plates and 54 Illustrations in the Text. Crown 8vo., 10s. 6d.

MOUNTAINEERING. By C. T. DENT. With Contributions by Sir W. M. CONWAY, D. W. FRESHFIELD, C. E. MATHEWS, &c. With 13 Plates and 95 Illustrations in the Text. Crown 8vo., 10s. 6d.

POETRY OF SPORT (THE).—Selected by HEDLEY PEEK. With a Chapter on Classical Allusions to Sport by ANDREW LANG, and a Special Preface to the Badminton Library by A. E. T. WATSON. With 32 Plates and 74 Illustrations in the Text. Crown 8vo., 10s. 6d.

RACING AND STEEPLE-CHASING. By the EARL OF SUFFOLK AND BERKSHIRE, W. G. CRAVEN, the HON. F. LAWLEY, ARTHUR COVENTRY, and A. E. T. WATSON. With Frontispiece and 56 Illustrations in the Text. Crown 8vo., 10s. 6d.

Sport and Pastime—*continued.*
THE BADMINTON LIBRARY—*continued.*

RIDING AND POLO. By Captain ROBERT WEIR, J. MORAY BROWN, T. F. DALE, the DUKE OF BEAUFORT, the EARL OF SUFFOLK AND BERKSHIRE, &c. With 18 Plates and 41 Illustrations in the Text. Crown 8vo., 10s. 6d.

ROWING. By R. P. P. ROWE and C. M. PITMAN. With Chapters on Steering by C. P. SEROCOLD, and F. C. BEGG; Metropolitan Rowing by S. LE BLANC SMITH; and on PUNTING by P. W. SQUIRE. With 75 Illustrations. Crown 8vo., 10s. 6d.

SEA FISHING. By JOHN BICKERDYKE, Sir H. W. GORE-BOOTH, ALFRED C. HARMSWORTH, and W. SENIOR. With 22 Full-page Plates and 175 Illustrations in the Text. Crown 8vo., 10s. 6d.

SHOOTING.

Vol. I. FIELD AND COVERT. By LORD WALSINGHAM and Sir RALPH PAYNE-GALLWEY, Bart. With Contributions by the Hon. GERALD LASCELLES and A. J. STUART-WORTLEY. With 11 Plates and 94 Illustrations in the Text. Crown 8vo., 10s. 6d.

Vol. II. MOOR AND MARSH. By LORD WALSINGHAM and Sir RALPH PAYNE-GALLWEY, Bart. With Contributions by LORD LOVAT and LORD CHARLES LENNOX KERR. With 8 Plates and 57 Illustrations in the Text. Crown 8vo., 10s. 6d.

SKATING, CURLING, TOBOGGANING. By J. M. HEATHCOTE, C. G. TEBBUTT, T. MAXWELL WITHAM, Rev. JOHN KERR, ORMOND HAKE, HENRY A. BUCK, &c. With 12 Plates and 272 Illustrations in the Text. Cr. 8vo., 10s. 6d.

SWIMMING. By ARCHIBALD SINCLAIR and WILLIAM HENRY, Hon. Secs of the Life-Saving Society. With 13 Plates and 106 Illustrations in the Text. Cr. 8vo., 10s. 6d.

TENNIS, LAWN TENNIS, RACKETS, AND FIVES. By J. M. and C. G. HEATHCOTE, E. O PLEYDELL-BOUVERIE, and A. C. AINGER. With Contributions by the Hon. A. LYTTELTON, W. C. MARSHALL, Miss L. DOD, &c. With 12 Plates and 67 Illustrations in the Text. Crown 8vo., 10s. 6d.

YACHTING.

Vol. I. CRUISING, CONSTRUCTION OF YACHTS, YACHT RACING RULES, FITTING-OUT, &c. By Sir EDWARD SULLIVAN, Bart., THE EARL OF PEMBROKE, LORD BRASSEY, K.C.B., C. E. SETH-SMITH, C.B., G. L. WATSON, R. T. PRITCHETT, E. F. KNIGHT, &c. With 21 Plates and 93 Illustrations in the Text. Crown 8vo., 10s. 6d.

Vol. II. YACHT CLUBS, YACHTING IN AMERICA AND THE COLONIES, YACHT RACING, &c. By R. T. PRITCHETT, THE MARQUIS OF DUFFERIN AND AVA, K.P., THE EARL OF ONSLOW, JAMES MCFERRAN, &c. With 35 Plates and 160 Illustrations in the Text. Crown 8vo., 10s. 6d.

FUR, FEATHER AND FIN SERIES.
Edited by A. E. T. WATSON.
Crown 8vo., price 5s. each Volume.
‚ *The Volumes are also issued half-bound in Leather, with gilt top. The price can be had from all Booksellers.*

THE PARTRIDGE. *Natural History*, by the Rev. H. A. MACPHERSON; *Shooting*, by A. J. STUART-WORTLEY; *Cookery*, by GEORGE SAINTSBURY. With 11 Illustrations and various Diagrams in the Text. Crown 8vo., 5s.

THE GROUSE. *Natural History*, by the Rev. H. A. MACPHERSON; *Shooting*, by A. J. STUART-WORTLEY; *Cookery*, by GEORGE SAINTSBURY. With 13 Illustrations and various Diagrams in the Text. Crown 8vo., 5s.

THE PHEASANT. *Natural History*, by the Rev. H. A. MACPHERSON; *Shooting*, by A. J. STUART-WORTLEY; *Cookery*, by ALEXANDER INNES SHAND. With 10 Illustrations and various Diagrams. Crown 8vo., 5s.

THE HARE. *Natural History*, by the Rev. H. A. MACPHERSON; *Shooting*, by the Hon. GERALD LASCELLES; *Coursing*, by CHARLES RICHARDSON; *Hunting*, by J. S. GIBBONS and G. H. LONGMAN; *Cookery*, by Col. KENNEY HERBERT. With 9 Illus. Cr. 8vo., 5s.

Sport and Pastime—*continued.*
FUR, FEATHER AND FIN SERIES—*continued.*

RED DEER *Natural History*, by the Rev. H. A. MACPHERSON; *Deer Stalking* by CAMERON OF LOCHIEL. *Stag Hunting*, by Viscount EBRINGTON; *Cookery*, by ALEXANDER INNES SHAND. With 10 Illustrations. Crown 8vo., 5s.

THE RABBIT. By JAMES EDMUND HARTING. With a Chapter on Cookery by ALEXANDER INNES SHAND. With 10 Illustrations. Crown 8vo., 5s.

WILDFOWL. By the Hon. JOHN SCOTT MONTAGU. With Illustrations, &c. [*In preparation.*

THE SALMON. By the Hon. A. E. GATHORNE-HARDY. With Chapters on the Law of Salmon-Fishing by CLAUD DOUGLAS PENNANT; Cookery, by ALEXANDER INNES SHAND. With 8 Illustrations. Crown 8vo., 5s.

THE TROUT. By the MARQUESS OF GRANBY. With Chapters on Breeding of Trout by Col. H. CUSTANCE; and Cookery, by ALEXANDER INNES SHAND. With 12 Illustrations. Crown 8vo., 5s.

André.—COLONEL BOGEY'S SKETCH-BOOK. Comprising an Eccentric Collection of Scribbles and Scratches found in disused Lockers and swept up in the Pavilion, together with sundry After-Dinner Sayings of the Colonel. By R. ANDRÉ, West Herts Golf Club. Oblong 4to., 2s. 6d.

Blackburne. — MR. BLACKBURNE'S GAMES AT CHESS. Selected, Annotated and Arranged by Himself. Edited, with a Biographical Sketch and a brief History of Blindfold Chess, by P. ANDERSON GRAHAM. 8vo., 7s. 6d. net.

DEAD SHOT (THE): or, Sportsman's Complete Guide. Being a Treatise on the Use of the Gun, with Rudimentary and Finishing Lessons in the Art of Shooting Game of all kinds. Also Game-driving, Wildfowl and Pigeon-shooting, Dog-breaking, etc. By MARKSMAN. With numerous Illustrations. Crown 8vo., 10s. 6d.

Ellis.—CHESS SPARKS; or, Short and Bright Games of Chess. Collected and Arranged by J. H. ELLIS, M.A. 8vo., 4s. 6d.

Folkard. — THE WILD-FOWLER: A Treatise on Fowling, Ancient and Modern; descriptive also of Decoys and Flight-ponds, Wild-fowl Shooting, Gunning-punts, Shooting-yachts, &c. Also Fowling in the Fens and in Foreign Countries, Rock-fowling, &c., &c., by H. C. FOLKARD. With 13 Engravings on Steel, and several Woodcuts. 8vo., 12s. 6d.

Ford.—THE THEORY AND PRACTICE OF ARCHERY. By HORACE FORD. New Edition, thoroughly Revised and Re-written by W. BUTT, M.A. With a Preface by C. J. LONGMAN, M.A. 8vo., 14s.

Francis.—A BOOK ON ANGLING: or, Treatise on the Art of Fishing in every Branch; including full Illustrated List of Salmon Flies. By FRANCIS FRANCIS. With Portrait and Coloured Plates. Crown 8vo., 15s.

Gibson.—TOBOGGANING ON CROOKED RUNS. By the Hon. HARRY GIBSON. With Contributions by F. DE B. STRICKLAND and 'LADY-TOBOGGANER'. With 40 Illustrations. Crown 8vo., 6s.

Graham.—COUNTRY PASTIMES FOR BOYS. By P. ANDERSON GRAHAM. With 252 Illustrations from Drawings and Photographs. Crown 8vo., 3s. 6d.

Hutchinson.—THE BOOK OF GOLF AND GOLFERS. By HORACE G. HUTCHINSON. With Contributions by Miss AMY PASCOE, H. H. HILTON, J. H. TAYLOR, H. J. WHIGHAM, and Messrs. SUTTON & SONS. With 71 Portraits, &c. Medium 8vo., 18s. net.

Lang.—ANGLING SKETCHES. By ANDREW LANG. With 20 Illustrations. Crown 8vo., 3s. 6d.

Lillie.—CROQUET: its History, Rules, and Secrets. By ARTHUR LILLIE, Champion Grand National Croquet Club, 1872; Winner of the 'All-Comers' Championship,' Maidstone, 1896. With 4 Full-page Illustrations by LUCIEN DAVIS, 15 Illustrations in the Text, and 27 Diagrams. Crown 8vo., 6s.

Longman.—CHESS OPENINGS. By FREDERICK W. LONGMAN. Fcp. 8vo., 2s. 6d.

Madden.—THE DIARY OF MASTER WILLIAM SILENCE: A Study of Shakespeare and of Elizabethan Sport. By the Right Hon. D. H. MADDEN, Vice-Chancellor of the University of Dublin. 8vo., 16s.

Sport and Pastime—*continued.*

Maskelyne.—SHARPS AND FLATS: a Complete Revelation of the Secrets of Cheating at Games of Chance and Skill. By JOHN NEVIL MASKELYNE, of the Egyption Hall. With 62 Illustrations. Crown 8vo., 6s.

Moffat.—CRICKETY CRICKET: Rhymes and Parodies. By DOUGLAS MOFFAT, with Frontispiece by Sir FRANK LOCKWOOD, Q.C., M.P., and 53 Illustrations by the Author. Crown 8vo., 2s. 6d.

Park.—THE GAME OF GOLF. By WILLIAM PARK, Junr., Champion Golfer, 1887-89. With 17 Plates and 26 Illustrations in the Text. Cr. 8vo., 7s. 6d.

Payne-Gallwey (Sir RALPH, Bart.).
LETTERS TO YOUNG SHOOTERS (First Series). On the Choice and Use of a Gun. With 41 Illustrations. Cr. 8vo., 7s. 6d.
LETTERS TO YOUNG SHOOTERS (Second Series). On the Production, Preservation, and Killing of Game. With Directions in Shooting Wood-Pigeons and Breaking-in Retrievers. With Portrait and 103 Illustrations. Crown 8vo., 12s. 6d.
LETTERS TO YOUNG SHOOTERS (Third Series). Comprising a Short Natural History of the Wildfowl that are Rare or Common to the British Islands, with Complete Directions in Shooting Wildfowl on the Coast and Inland. With 200 Illustrations. Cr. 8vo., 18s.

Pole.—THE THEORY OF THE MODERN SCIENTIFIC GAME OF WHIST. By WILLIAM POLE, F.R.S. Fcp. 8vo., 2s. 6d.

Proctor.—HOW TO PLAY WHIST: WITH THE LAWS AND ETIQUETTE OF WHIST. By RICHARD A. PROCTOR. Crown 8vo., 3s. 6d.

Ribblesdale.—THE QUEEN'S HOUNDS AND STAG-HUNTING RECOLLECTIONS. By LORD RIBBLESDALE, Master of the Buckhounds, 1892-95. With Introductory Chapter on the Hereditary Mastership by E. BURROWS. With 24 Plates and 35 Illustrations in the Text. 8vo., 25s.

Ronalds.—THE FLY-FISHER'S ENTOMOLOGY. By ALFRED RONALDS. With 20 Coloured Plates. 8vo., 14s.

Watson.—RACING AND 'CHASING: a Collection of Sporting Stories. By ALFRED E. T. WATSON, Editor of the 'Badminton Magazine'. With 16 Plates and 36 Illustrations in the Text. Crown 8vo., 7s. 6d.

Wilcocks. THE SEA FISHERMAN: Comprising the Chief Methods of Hook and Line Fishing in the British and other Seas, and Remarks on Nets, Boats, and Boating. By J. C. WILCOCKS. Illustrated. Crown 8vo., 6s.

Veterinary Medicine, &c.

Steel (JOHN HENRY, F.R.C.V.S., F.Z.S., A.V.D.), late Professor of Veterinary Science and Principal of Bombay Veterinary College.
A TREATISE ON THE DISEASES OF THE DOG: being a Manual of Canine Pathology. Especially adapted for the use of Veterinary Practitioners and Students. With 88 Illus. 8vo., 10s. 6d.
A TREATISE ON THE DISEASES OF THE OX: being a Manual of Bovine Pathology. Especially adapted for the use of Veterinary Practitioners and Students. With 2 Plates and 117 Woodcuts. 8vo., 15s.
A TREATISE ON THE DISEASES OF THE SHEEP: being a Manual of Ovine Pathology for the use of Veterinary Practitioners and Students. With Coloured Plate and 99 Woodcuts. 8vo., 12s.
OUTLINES OF EQUINE ANATOMY: a Manual for the use of Veterinary Students in the Dissecting Room. Crown 8vo., 7s. 6d.

Fitzwygram.—HORSES AND STABLES. By Major-General Sir F. FITZWYGRAM, Bart. With 56 pages of Illustrations. 8vo., 2s. 6d. net.

Schreiner. — THE ANGORA GOAT (published under the auspices of the South African Angora Goat Breeders' Association), and a Paper on the Ostrich (reprinted from the *Zoologist* for March, 1897). With 26 Illustrations. By S. C. CRONWRIGHT SCHREINER. 8vo., 10s. 6d.

'Stonehenge.'—THE DOG IN HEALTH AND DISEASE. By 'STONEHENGE'. With 78 Wood Engravings. 8vo., 7s. 6d.

Youatt (WILLIAM).
THE HORSE. Revised and enlarged. By W. WATSON, M.R.C.V.S. With 52 Wood Engravings. 8vo., 7s. 6d.
THE DOG. Revised and enlarged. With 33 Wood Engravings. 8vo., 6s.

Mental, Moral, and Political Philosophy.
LOGIC, RHETORIC, PSYCHOLOGY, &c.

Abbott.—THE ELEMENTS OF LOGIC. By T. K. ABBOTT, B.D. 12mo., 3s.

Aristotle.
THE ETHICS: Greek Text, Illustrated with Essay and Notes. By Sir ALEXANDER GRANT, Bart. 2 vols. 8vo., 32s.
AN INTRODUCTION TO ARISTOTLE'S ETHICS. Books I.-IV. (Book X. c. vi.-ix. in an Appendix.) With a continuous Analysis and Notes. By the Rev. E. MOORE, D.D. Cr. 8vo., 10s. 6d.

Bacon (FRANCIS).
COMPLETE WORKS. Edited by R. L. ELLIS, JAMES SPEDDING, and D. D. HEATH. 7 vols. 8vo., £3 13s. 6d.
LETTERS AND LIFE, including all his occasional Works. Edited by JAMES SPEDDING. 7 vols. 8vo., £4 4s.
THE ESSAYS: with Annotations. By RICHARD WHATELY, D.D. 8vo., 10s. 6d.
THE ESSAYS: Edited, with Notes. By F. STORR and C. H. GIBSON. Cr. 8vo., 3s. 6d.
THE ESSAYS. With Introduction, Notes, and Index. By E. A. ABBOTT, D.D. 2 vols. Fcp 8vo., 6s. The Text and Index only, without Introduction and Notes, in One Volume. Fcp. 8vo., 2s. 6d.

Bain (ALEXANDER).
MENTAL SCIENCE. Crown 8vo., 6s. 6d.
MORAL SCIENCE. Crown 8vo., 4s. 6d.
The two works as above can be had in one volume, price 10s. 6d.
SENSES AND THE INTELLECT. 8vo., 15s.
EMOTIONS AND THE WILL. 8vo., 15s.
LOGIC, DEDUCTIVE AND INDUCTIVE. Part I., 4s. Part II., 6s. 6d.
PRACTICAL ESSAYS. Crown 8vo., 2s.

Bray.—THE PHILOSOPHY OF NECESSITY; or Law in Mind as in Matter. By CHARLES BRAY. Crown 8vo., 5s.

Crozier (JOHN BEATTIE).
HISTORY OF INTELLECTUAL DEVELOPMENT: on the Lines of Modern Evolution.
Vol. I. Greek and Hindoo Thought; Græco-Roman Paganism; Judaism; and Christianity down to the Closing of the Schools of Athens by Justinian, 529 A.D. 8vo., 14s.

Crozier (JOHN BEATTIE)—*continued.*
CIVILISATION AND PROGRESS; being the Outlines of a New System of Political, Religious and Social Philosophy. 8vo., 14s.

Davidson.—THE LOGIC OF DEFINITION, Explained and Applied. By WILLIAM L. DAVIDSON, M.A. Crown 8vo., 6s.

Green (THOMAS HILL). The Works of. Edited by R. L. NETTLESHIP.
Vols. I. and II. Philosophical Works. 8vo., 16s. each.
Vol. III. Miscellanies. With Index to the three Volumes, and Memoir. 8vo., 21s.
LECTURES ON THE PRINCIPLES OF POLITICAL OBLIGATION. With Preface by BERNARD BOSANQUET. 8vo., 5s.

Hodgson (SHADWORTH H.).
TIME AND SPACE: a Metaphysical Essay. 8vo., 16s.
THE THEORY OF PRACTICE · an Ethical Inquiry. 2 vols. 8vo., 24s.
THE PHILOSOPHY OF REFLECTION. 2 vols. 8vo., 21s.
THE METAPHYSIC OF EXPERIENCE. Book I. General Analysis of Experience. Book II. Positive Science. Book III. Analysis of Conscious Action. Book IV. The Real Universe. 4 vols. 8vo., 36s. net.

Hume.—THE PHILOSOPHICAL WORKS OF DAVID HUME. Edited by T. H. GREEN and T. H. GROSE. 4 vols. 8vo., 28s. Or separately, Essays. 2 vols. 14s. Treatise of Human Nature. 2 vols. 14s.

James.—THE WILL TO BELIEVE, and other Essays in Popular Philosophy. By WILLIAM JAMES, M.D., LL.D., &c. Crown 8vo., 7s. 6d.

Justinian.—THE INSTITUTES OF JUSTINIAN: Latin Text, chiefly that of Huschke, with English Introduction, Translation, Notes, and Summary. By THOMAS C. SANDARS, M.A. 8vo., 18s.

Kant (IMMANUEL).
CRITIQUE OF PRACTICAL REASON, AND OTHER WORKS ON THE THEORY OF ETHICS. Translated by T. K. ABBOTT, B.D. With Memoir. 8vo., 12s. 6d.

Mental, Moral and Political Philosophy—*continued.*

Kant (IMMANUEL)—*continued.*

FUNDAMENTAL PRINCIPLES OF THE METAPHYSIC OF ETHICS. Translated by T. K. ABBOTT, B.D. Crown 8vo., 3*s.*

INTRODUCTION TO LOGIC, AND HIS ESSAY ON THE MISTAKEN SUBTILTY OF THE FOUR FIGURES. Translated by T. K. ABBOTT. 8vo., 6*s.*

Killick.—HANDBOOK TO MILL'S SYSTEM OF LOGIC. By Rev. A. H. KILLICK, M.A. Crown 8vo., 3*s.* 6*d.*

Ladd (GEORGE TRUMBULL).

A THEORY OF REALITY: an Essay in Metaphysical System upon the Basis of Human Cognitive Experience. 8vo., 18*s.*

ELEMENTS OF PHYSIOLOGICAL PSYCHOLOGY. 8vo., 21*s.*

OUTLINES OF DESCRIPTIVE PSYCHOLOGY: a Text-Book of Mental Science for Colleges and Normal Schools. 8vo., 12*s.*

OUTLINES OF PHYSIOLOGICAL PSYCHOLOGY. 8vo., 12*s.*

PRIMER OF PSYCHOLOGY. Crown 8vo., 5*s.* 6*d.*

Lecky.—THE MAP OF LIFE: CONDUCT AND CHARACTER. By WILLIAM EDWARD HARTPOLE LECKY. 8vo., 10*s.* 6*d.*

Lutoslawski.—THE ORIGIN AND GROWTH OF PLATO'S LOGIC. With an Account of Plato's Style and of the Chronology of his Writings. By WINCENTY LUTOSLAWSKI. 8vo., 21*s.*

Max Müller (F.).

THE SCIENCE OF THOUGHT. 8vo., 21*s.*

THE SIX SYSTEMS OF INDIAN PHILOSOPHY. 8vo., 18*s.*

Mill.—ANALYSIS OF THE PHENOMENA OF THE HUMAN MIND. By JAMES MILL. 2 vols. 8vo., 28*s.*

Mill (JOHN STUART).

A SYSTEM OF LOGIC. Cr. 8vo., 3*s.* 6*d.*

ON LIBERTY. Cr. 8vo., 1*s.* 4*d.*

CONSIDERATIONS ON REPRESENTATIVE GOVERNMENT. Crown 8vo., 2*s.*

UTILITARIANISM. 8vo., 2*s.* 6*d.*

Mill (JOHN STUART)—*continued.*

EXAMINATION OF SIR WILLIAM HAMILTON'S PHILOSOPHY. 8vo., 16*s.*

NATURE, THE UTILITY OF RELIGION, AND THEISM. Three Essays. 8vo., 5*s.*

Monck.—AN INTRODUCTION TO LOGIC. By WILLIAM HENRY S. MONCK, M.A. Crown 8vo., 5*s.*

Romanes.—MIND AND MOTION AND MONISM. By GEORGE JOHN ROMANES, LL.D., F.R.S. Crown 8vo., 4*s.* 6*d.*

Stock.—LECTURES IN THE LYCEUM; or, Aristotle's Ethics for English Readers. Edited by ST. GEORGE STOCK. Crown 8vo., 7*s.* 6*d.*

Sully (JAMES).

THE HUMAN MIND: a Text-book of Psychology. 2 vols. 8vo., 21*s.*

OUTLINES OF PSYCHOLOGY. Crown 8vo., 9*s.*

THE TEACHER'S HANDBOOK OF PSYCHOLOGY. Crown 8vo., 6*s.* 6*d.*

STUDIES OF CHILDHOOD. 8vo. 10*s.* 6*d.*

CHILDREN'S WAYS: being Selections from the Author's 'Studies of Childhood'. With 25 Illustrations. Crown 8vo., 4*s.* 6*d.*

Sutherland. — THE ORIGIN AND GROWTH OF THE MORAL INSTINCT. By ALEXANDER SUTHERLAND, M.A. 2 vols. 8vo., 28*s.*

Swinburne.—PICTURE LOGIC: an Attempt to Popularise the Science of Reasoning. By ALFRED JAMES SWINBURNE, M.A. Crown 8vo., 2*s.* 6*d.*

Webb.—THE VEIL OF ISIS: a Series of Essays on Idealism. By THOMAS E. WEBB, LL.D., Q.C. 8vo., 10*s.* 6*d.*

Weber.—HISTORY OF PHILOSOPHY. By ALFRED WEBER, Professor in the University of Strasburg. Translated by FRANK THILLY, Ph.D. 8vo., 16*s.*

Whately (ARCHBISHOP).

BACON'S ESSAYS. With Annotations. 8vo., 10*s.* 6*d.*

ELEMENTS OF LOGIC. Cr. 8vo., 4*s.* 6*d.*

ELEMENTS OF RHETORIC. Cr. 8vo., 4*s.* 6*d.*

Mental, Moral and Political Philosophy—*continued.*

Zeller (Dr. EDWARD).

THE STOICS, EPICUREANS, AND SCEP-
TICS. Translated by the Rev. O. J.
REICHEL, M.A. Crown 8vo., 15*s.*

OUTLINES OF THE HISTORY OF GREEK
PHILOSOPHY. Translated by SARAH
F. ALLEYNE and EVELYN ABBOTT,
M.A., LL.D. Crown 8vo., 10*s.* 6*d.*

Zeller (Dr. EDWARD)—*continued.*
PLATO AND THE OLDER ACADEMY.
Translated by SARAH F. ALLEYNE
and ALFRED GOODWIN, B.A. Crown
8vo., 18*s.*
SOCRATES AND THE SOCRATIC SCHOOLS.
Translated by the Rev. O. J. REICHEL,
M.A. Crown 8vo., 10*s.* 6*d.*
ARISTOTLE AND THE EARLIER PERI-
PATETICS. Translated by B. F. C.
COSTELLOE, M.A., and J. H. MUIR-
HEAD, M.A. 2 vols. Cr. 8vo., 24*s.*

MANUALS OF CATHOLIC PHILOSOPHY.

(Stonyhurst Series.)

A MANUAL OF POLITICAL ECONOMY.
By C. S. DEVAS, M.A. Cr. 8vo., 6*s.* 6*d.*

FIRST PRINCIPLES OF KNOWLEDGE. By
JOHN RICKABY, S.J. Crown 8vo., 5*s.*

GENERAL METAPHYSICS. By JOHN RICK-
ABY, S.J. Crown 8vo., 5*s.*

LOGIC. By RICHARD F. CLARKE, S.J.
Crown 8vo., 5*s.*

MORAL PHILOSOPHY (ETHICS AND NATU-
RAL LAW). By JOSEPH RICKABY, S.J.
Crown 8vo., 5*s.*

NATURAL THEOLOGY. By BERNARD
BOEDDER, S.J. Crown 8vo., 6*s.* 6*d.*

PSYCHOLOGY. By MICHAEL MAHER,
S.J. Crown 8vo., 6*s.* 6*d.*

History and Science of Language, &c.

Davidson.—LEADING AND IMPORTANT
ENGLISH WORDS: Explained and Ex-
emplified. By WILLIAM L. DAVID-
SON, M.A. Fcp. 8vo., 3*s.* 6*d.*

Farrar.—LANGUAGE AND LANGUAGES.
By F. W. FARRAR, D.D., Dean of
Canterbury. Crown 8vo., 6*s.*

Graham.—ENGLISH SYNONYMS, Classified and Explained : with Practical
Exercises. By G. F. GRAHAM. Fcap.
8vo., 6*s.*

Max Müller (F.).
THE SCIENCE OF LANGUAGE, Founded
on Lectures delivered at the Royal
Institution in 1861 and 1863. 2 vols.
Crown 8vo., 10*s.*
BIOGRAPHIES OF WORDS, AND THE
HOME OF THE ARYAS. Crown 8vo.,
5*s.*

Roget. — THESAURUS OF ENGLISH
WORDS AND PHRASES. Classified and
Arranged so as to Facilitate the Ex-
pression of Ideas and assist in Literary
Composition. By PETER MARK ROGET,
M.D., F.R.S. With full Index. Crown
8vo., 10*s.* 6*d.*

Whately.—ENGLISH SYNONYMS. By
E. JANE WHATELY. Fcap. 8vo., 3*s.*

Political Economy and Economics.

Ashley.—ENGLISH ECONOMIC HISTORY AND THEORY. By W. J. ASHLEY, M.A. Cr. 8vo., Part I., 5s. Part II., 10s. 6d.

Bagehot.—ECONOMIC STUDIES. By WALTER BAGEHOT. Cr. 8vo., 3s. 6d.

Brassey.—PAPERS AND ADDRESSES ON WORK AND WAGES. By Lord BRASSEY. Edited by J POTTER, and with Introduction by GEORGE HOWELL, M.P. Crown 8vo., 5s.

Channing.—THE TRUTH ABOUT AGRICULTURAL DEPRESSION: An Economic Study of the Evidence of the Royal Commission. By FRANCIS ALLSTON CHANNING, M.P., one of the Commission. Crown 8vo., 6s.

Devas.—A MANUAL OF POLITICAL ECONOMY. By C. S. DEVAS, M.A. Crown 8vo., 6s. 6d. (*Manuals of Catholic Philosophy.*)

Jordan.—THE STANDARD OF VALUE. By WILLIAM LEIGHTON JORDAN. Crown 8vo., 6s.

Leslie.—ESSAYS ON POLITICAL ECONOMY. By T. E. CLIFFE LESLIE, Hon. LL.D., Dubl. 8vo., 10s. 6d.

Macleod (HENRY DUNNING).
ECONOMICS FOR BEGINNERS. Crown 8vo., 2s.
THE ELEMENTS OF ECONOMICS. 2 vols. Crown 8vo., 3s. 6d. each.
BIMETALISM. 8vo., 5s. net.
THE ELEMENTS OF BANKING. Crown 8vo., 3s. 6d.
THE THEORY AND PRACTICE OF BANKING. Vol. I. 8vo., 12s. Vol. II. 14s.

Macleod (HENRY DUNNING)—*cont.*
THE THEORY OF CREDIT. 8vo. In 1 Vol., 30s. net; or separately, Vol. I. 10s. net. Vol. II., Part I., 10s. net. Vol. II. Part II., 10s. net.

Mill.—POLITICAL ECONOMY. By JOHN STUART MILL.
Popular Edition. Crown 8vo., 3s 6d.
Library Edition. 2 vols. 8vo., 30s

Mulhall.—INDUSTRIES AND WEALTH OF NATIONS. By MICHAEL G. MULHALL, F.S.S. With 32 Diagrams. Cr. 8vo., 8s. 6d.

Stephens.—HIGHER LIFE FOR WORKING PEOPLE: its Hindrances Discussed. An attempt to solve some pressing Social Problems, without injustice to Capital or Labour. By W. WALKER STEPHENS. Crown 8vo., 3s. 6d.

Symes.—POLITICAL ECONOMY. With a Supplementary Chapter on Socialism. By J. E. SYMES, M.A. Crown 8vo., 2s. 6d.

Toynbee.—LECTURES ON THE INDUSTRIAL REVOLUTION OF THE 18th CENTURY IN ENGLAND. By ARNOLD TOYNBEE. With a Memoir of the Author by BENJAMIN JOWETT, D.D. 8vo., 10s. 6d.

Webb (SIDNEY and BEATRICE).
THE HISTORY OF TRADE UNIONISM. With Map and full Bibliography of the Subject. 8vo., 18s.
INDUSTRIAL DEMOCRACY: a Study in Trade Unionism. 2 vols. 8vo., 25s. net.
PROBLEMS OF MODERN INDUSTRY: Essays. 8vo., 7s. 6d.

Wright. — OUTLINE OF PRACTICAL SOCIOLOGY. With Special Reference to American Conditions. By CARROLL D. WRIGHT, LL.D With 12 Maps and Diagrams. Crown 8vo., 9s

STUDIES IN ECONOMICS AND POLITICAL SCIENCE.

Issued under the auspices of the London School of Economics and Political Science.

GERMAN SOCIAL DEMOCRACY. By BERTRAND RUSSELL, B.A. With an Appendix on Social Democracy and the Woman Question in Germany by ALYS RUSSELL, B.A. Cr. 8vo., 3s. 6d.

THE REFERENDUM IN SWITZERLAND. By SIMON DEPLOIGE, Advocate. Translated by C. P. TREVELYAN, M.P. Edited with Notes, Introduction and Appendices, by LILIAN TOMN. Crown 8vo., 7s. 6d.

THE HISTORY OF LOCAL RATES IN ENGLAND: Five Lectures. By EDWIN CANNAN, M.A. Crown 8vo., 2s. 6d.

LOCAL VARIATIONS IN WAGES. By F. W. LAWRENCE, M.A., Fellow of Trinity College, Cambridge. Medium 4to., 8s. 6d.

THE ECONOMIC POLICY OF COLBERT. By A. J. SARGENT, B.A., Senior Hulme Exhibitioner of Brasenose College, Oxford. Crown 8vo., 2s. 6d.

SELECT DOCUMENTS ILLUSTRATING THE HISTORY OF TRADE UNIONISM.
1. The Tailoring Trade. Edited by W. F. GALTON. With a Preface by SIDNEY WEBB, LL.B. Crown 8vo., 5s.

Evolution, Anthropology, &c.

Clodd (EDWARD).

THE STORY OF CREATION : a Plain Account of Evolution. With 77 Illustrations. Crown 8vo., 3s. 6d.

A PRIMER OF EVOLUTION : being a Popular Abridged Edition of 'The Story of Creation'. With Illustrations. Fcp. 8vo., 1s. 6d.

Lang (ANDREW).

CUSTOM AND MYTH : Studies of Early Usage and Belief. With 15 Illustrations. Crown 8vo., 3s. 6d.

MYTH, RITUAL, AND RELIGION. 2 vols. Crown 8vo., 7s.

Lubbock.—THE ORIGIN OF CIVILISATION and the Primitive Condition of Man. By Sir J. LUBBOCK, Bart., M.P. With 5 Plates and 20 Illustrations. 8vo., 18s.

Romanes (GEORGE JOHN).

DARWIN, AND AFTER DARWIN : an Exposition of the Darwinian Theory, and a Discussion on Post-Darwinian Questions.

Part I. THE DARWINIAN THEORY. With Portrait of Darwin and 125 Illustrations. Crown 8vo., 10s. 6d.

Part II. POST-DARWINIAN QUESTIONS : Heredity and Utility. With Portrait of the Author and 5 Illustrations. Cr. 8vo., 10s. 6d.

Part III. POST-DARWINIAN QUESTIONS : Isolation and Physiological Selection. Crown 8vo., 5s.

AN EXAMINATION OF WEISMANNISM. Crown 8vo., 6s.

ESSAYS. Edited by C. LLOYD MORGAN, Principal of University College, Bristol. Crown 8vo., 6s.

Classical Literature, Translations, &c.

Abbott.—HELLENICA. A Collection of Essays on Greek Poetry, Philosophy, History, and Religion. Edited by EVELYN ABBOTT, M.A., LL.D. Crown 8vo., 7s. 6d.

Æschylus.—EUMENIDES OF ÆSCHYLUS. With Metrical English Translation. By J. F. DAVIES. 8vo., 7s.

Aristophanes.—The ACHARNIANS OF ARISTOPHANES, translated into English Verse. By R. Y. TYRRELL. Cr. 8vo., 1s.

Aristotle.—YOUTH AND OLD AGE, LIFE AND DEATH, AND RESPIRATION. Translated, with Introduction and Notes, by W. OGLE, M.A., M.D. 8vo., 7s. 6d.

Becker (W. A.). Translated by the Rev. F. Metcalfe, B.D.

GALLUS : or, Roman Scenes in the Time of Augustus. With Notes and Excursuses. With 26 Illustrations. Post 8vo., 3s. 6d.

CHARICLES : or, Illustrations of the Private Life of the Ancient Greeks. With Notes and Excursuses. With 26 Illustrations. Post 8vo., 3s. 6d.

Butler.—THE AUTHORESS OF THE ODYSSEY, WHERE AND WHEN SHE WROTE, WHO SHE WAS, THE USE SHE MADE OF THE ILIAD, AND HOW THE POEM GREW UNDER HER HANDS. By SAMUEL BUTLER, Author of 'Erewhon,' &c. With Illustrations and 4 Maps. 8vo., 10s. 6d.

Cicero.—CICERO'S CORRESPONDENCE. By R. Y. TYRRELL. Vols. I., II., III. 8vo., each 12s. Vol. IV., 15s. Vol. V., 14s. Vol. VI., 12s.

Homer.

THE ILIAD OF HOMER. Rendered into English Prose for the use of those that cannot read the original. By SAMUEL BUTLER, Author of 'Erewhon,' etc. Crown 8vo., 7s. 6d.

THE ODYSSEY OF HOMER. Done into English Verse. By WILLIAM MORRIS. Crown 8vo., 6s.

Horace.—THE WORKS OF HORACE, rendered into English Prose. With Life, Introduction, and Notes. By WILLIAM COUTTS, M.A. Crown 8vo., 5s. net.

Classical Literature, Translations, &c.—*continued.*

Lang.—HOMER AND THE EPIC. By ANDREW LANG. Crown 8vo., 9*s*. net.

Lucan.—THE PHARSALIA OF LUCAN. Translated into Blank Verse. By Sir EDWARD RIDLEY. 8vo., 14*s*.

Mackail.—SELECT EPIGRAMS FROM THE GREEK ANTHOLOGY. By J. W. MACKAIL. Edited with a Revised Text, Introduction, Translation, and Notes. 8vo., 16*s*.

Rich.—A DICTIONARY OF ROMAN AND GREEK ANTIQUITIES. By A. RICH, B.A. With 2000 Woodcuts. Crown 8vo., 7*s*. 6*d*.

Sophocles.—Translated into English Verse. By ROBERT WHITELAW, M.A., Assistant Master in Rugby School. Cr. 8vo., 8*s*. 6*d*.

Tyrrell.—DUBLIN TRANSLATIONS INTO GREEK AND LATIN VERSE. Edited by R. Y. TYRRELL. 8vo., 6*s*.

Virgil.

THE ÆNEID OF VIRGIL. Translated into English Verse by JOHN CONINGTON. Crown 8vo., 6*s*.

THE POEMS OF VIRGIL. Translated into English Prose by JOHN CONINGTON. Crown 8vo., 6*s*.

THE ÆNEIDS OF VIRGIL. Done into English Verse. By WILLIAM MORRIS. Crown 8vo., 6*s*.

THE ÆNEID OF VIRGIL, freely translated into English Blank Verse. By W. J. THORNHILL. Crown 8vo., 7*s*. 6*d*.

THE ÆNEID OF VIRGIL. Translated into English Verse by JAMES RHOADES.
Books I.- VI. Crown 8vo., 5*s*.
Books VII.-XII. Crown 8vo., 5*s*.

THE ECLOGUES AND GEORGICS OF VIRGIL. Translated into English Prose by J. W. MACKAIL, Fellow of Balliol College, Oxford. 16mo., 5*s*.

Wilkins.—THE GROWTH OF THE HOMERIC POEMS. By G. WILKINS. 8vo., 6*s*.

Poetry and the Drama.

Armstrong (G. F. SAVAGE).

POEMS: Lyrical and Dramatic. Fcp. 8vo., 6*s*.

KING SAUL. (The Tragedy of Israel, Part I.) Fcp. 8vo., 5*s*.

KING DAVID. (The Tragedy of Israel, Part II.) Fcp. 8vo., 6*s*.

KING SOLOMON. (The Tragedy of Israel, Part III.) Fcp. 8vo., 6*s*.

UGONE: a Tragedy. Fcp. 8vo., 6*s*.

A GARLAND FROM GREECE: Poems Fcp. 8vo., 7*s*. 6*d*.

STORIES OF WICKLOW: Poems. Fcp. 8vo., 7*s*. 6*d*.

MEPHISTOPHELES IN BROADCLOTH: a Satire. Fcp. 8vo., 4*s*.

ONE IN THE INFINITE: a Poem. Cr. 8vo., 7*s*. 6*d*.

Armstrong.—THE POETICAL WORKS OF EDMUND J. ARMSTRONG. Fcp. 8vo., 5*s*.

Arnold.—THE LIGHT OF THE WORLD: or, the Great Consummation. By Sir EDWIN ARNOLD. With 14 Illustrations after HOLMAN HUNT. Crown 8vo., 6*s*.

Barraud.—THE LAY OF THE KNIGHTS. By the Rev. C. W. BARRAUD, S.J., Author of 'St. Thomas of Canterbury, and other Poems'. Crown 8vo., 4*s*.

Bell (Mrs. HUGH).

CHAMBER COMEDIES: a Collection of Plays and Monologues for the Drawing Room. Crown 8vo., 6*s*.

FAIRY TALE PLAYS, AND HOW TO ACT THEM. With 91 Diagrams and 52 Illustrations. Crown 8vo., 3*s*. 6*d*.

· Poetry and the Drama—*continued*.

Coleridge.—SELECTIONS FROM. With Introduction by ANDREW LANG. With 18 Illustrations by PATTEN WILSON. Crown 8vo., 3*s.* 6*d.*

Goethe.—THE FIRST PART OF THE TRAGEDY OF FAUST IN ENGLISH. By THOS. E. WEBB, LL.D., sometime Fellow of Trinity College; Professor of Moral Philosophy in the University of Dublin, etc. New and Cheaper Edition, with THE DEATH OF FAUST, from the Second Part. Crown 8vo., 6*s.*

Gore-Booth.—POEMS. By EVA GORE-BOOTH. Fcp. 8vo., 5*s.*

Ingelow (JEAN).

POETICAL WORKS. Complete in One Volume. Crown 8vo., 7*s.* 6*d.*

LYRICAL AND OTHER POEMS. Selected from the Writings of JEAN INGELOW. Fcp. 8vo., 2*s.* 6*d.*; cloth plain, 3*s.* cloth gilt.

Lang (ANDREW).

GRASS OF PARNASSUS. Fcp. 8vo., 2*s.* 6*d.* net.

THE BLUE POETRY BOOK. Edited by ANDREW LANG. With 100 Illustrations. Crown 8vo., 6*s.*

Layard and Corder. — SONGS IN MANY MOODS. By NINA F. LAYARD; THE WANDERING ALBATROSS, &C. By ANNIE CORDER. In one volume. Crown 8vo., 5*s.*

Lecky.—POEMS. By the Rt. Hon. W. E. H. LECKY. Fcp. 8vo., 5*s.*

Lytton (THE EARL OF) (OWEN MEREDITH).

THE WANDERER. Cr. 8vo., 10*s.* 6*d.*

LUCILE. Crown 8vo., 10*s.* 6*d.*

SELECTED POEMS. Cr. 8vo., 10*s.* 6*d.*

Macaulay.—LAYS OF ANCIENT ROME, WITH 'IVRY,' AND 'THE ARMADA'. By Lord MACAULAY.

Illustrated by G. SCHARF. Fcp. 4to., 10*s.* 6*d.*

———————————— Bijou Edition. 18mo., 2*s.* 6*d.*, gilt top.

———————————— Popular Edition. Fcp. 4to., 6*d.* sewed, 1*s.* cloth.

Illustrated by J. R. WEGUELIN. Crown 8vo., 3*s.* 6*d.*

Annotated Edition. Fcp. 8vo., 1*s.* sewed, 1*s.* 6*d.* cloth.

MacDonald (GEORGE, LL.D.).

A BOOK OF STRIFE, IN THE FORM OF THE DIARY OF AN OLD SOUL: Poems. 18mo., 6*s.*

RAMPOLLI: GROWTHS FROM A LONG-PLANTED ROOT; being Translations, new and old (mainly in verse), chiefly from the German; along with 'A Year's Diary of an Old Soul'. Crown 8vo., 6*s.*

Moffat.—CRICKETY CRICKET: Rhymes and Parodies. By DOUGLAS MOFFAT. With Frontispiece by Sir FRANK LOCK-WOOD, Q.C., M.P., and 53 Illustrations by the Author. Crown 8vo., 2*s.* 6*d.*

Moon.—POEMS OF LOVE AND HOME, etc. By GEORGE WASHINGTON MOON, Hon. F.R.S.L., Author of 'Elijah,' etc. 16mo., 2*s.* 6*d.*

Morris (WILLIAM).

POETICAL WORKS—LIBRARY EDITION. Complete in Eleven Volumes. Crown 8vo., price 6*s.* each.

THE EARTHLY PARADISE. 4 vols. 6*s.* each.

THE LIFE AND DEATH OF JASON. 6*s.*

THE DEFENCE OF GUENEVERE, and other Poems. 6*s.*

THE STORY OF SIGURD THE VOLSUNG, and the Fall of the Niblungs. 6*s.*

LOVE IS ENOUGH; or, The Freeing of Pharamond: a Morality; and POEMS BY THE WAY 6*s.*

Poetry and the Drama—*continued.*

Morris (WILLIAM)—*continued.*

THE ODYSSEY OF HOMER. Done into English Verse. 6s.

THE ÆNEIDS OF VIRGIL. Done into English Verse. 6s.

THE TALE OF BEOWULF, SOMETIME KING OF THE FOLK OF THE WEDER-GEATS. Translated by WILLIAM MORRIS and A. J. WYATT. Crown 8vo., 6s.

Certain of the Poetical Works may also be had in the following Editions :—

THE EARTHLY PARADISE.

Popular Edition. 5 vols. 12mo., 25s. ; or 5s. each, sold separately.

The same in Ten Parts, 25s. ; or 2s. 6d. each, sold separately.

Cheap Edition, in 1 vol. Cr. 8vo., 7s. 6d.

POEMS BY THE WAY. Square crown 8vo., 6s.

** For Mr. William Morris's Prose Works, see pp. 22 and 31.

Nesbit.—LAYS AND LEGENDS. By E. NESBIT (Mrs. HUBERT BLAND). First Series. Crown 8vo., 3s. 6d. Second Series, with Portrait. Crown 8vo., 5s.

Rankin. — WAGNER'S NIBELUNGEN RING. Done into English Verse by REGINALD RANKIN, B.A., of the Inner Temple, Barrister-at-Law. Vol. I. Rhinegold and Valkyrie.

Riley (JAMES WHITCOMB).

OLD FASHIONED ROSES : Poems. 12mo., 5s.

RUBÁIYÁT OF DOC SIFERS. With 43 Illustrations by C. M. RELYEA. Crown 8vo.

THE GOLDEN YEAR. From the Verse and Prose of JAMES WHITCOMB RILEY. Compiled by CLARA E. LAUGHLIN. Fcp. 8vo., 5s.

Romanes.—A SELECTION FROM THE POEMS OF GEORGE JOHN ROMANES, M.A., LL.D., F.R.S. With an Introduction by T. HERBERT WARREN, President of Magdalen College, Oxford. Crown 8vo., 4s. 6d.

Russell.—SONNETS ON THE SONNET : an Anthology. Compiled by the Rev. MATTHEW RUSSELL, S.J. Crown 8vo., 3s 6d.

Samuels. — SHADOWS, AND OTHER POEMS. By E. SAMUELS. With 7 Illustrations by W. FITZGERALD, M.A. Crown 8vo., 3s. 6d.

Shakespeare.—BOWDLER'S FAMILY SHAKESPEARE. With 36 Woodcuts. 1 vol. 8vo., 14s. Or in 6 vols. Fcp. 8vo., 21s.

SHAKESPEARE'S SONNETS. Reconsidered, and in part Rearranged, with Introductory Chapters and a Reprint of the Original 1609 Edition. By SAMUEL BUTLER, Author of 'Erewhon,' etc.

THE SHAKESPEARE BIRTHDAY BOOK. By MARY F. DUNBAR. 32mo., 1s. 6d.

Wordsworth. — SELECTED POEMS. By ANDREW LANG. With Photogravure Frontispiece of Rydal Mount. With 16 Illustrations and numerous Initial Letters. By ALFRED PARSONS, A.R.A. Crown 8vo., gilt edges, 3s. 6d.

Wordsworth and Coleridge.—A DESCRIPTION OF THE WORDSWORTH AND COLERIDGE MANUSCRIPTS IN THE POSSESSION OF Mr. T. NORTON LONGMAN. Edited, with Notes, by W. HALE WHITE. With 3 Facsimile Reproductions. 4to., 10s. 6d.

Fiction, Humour, &c.

Anstey.—VOCES POPULI. Reprinted from 'Punch'. By F. ANSTEY, Author of 'Vice Versâ'. First Series. With 20 Illustrations by J. BERNARD PARTRIDGE. Crown 8vo., 3s. 6d.

Beaconsfield (THE EARL OF).

NOVELS AND TALES. Complete in 11 vols. Crown 8vo., 1s. 6d. each.

Vivian Grey.	Sybil.
The Young Duke, &c.	Henrietta Temple
Alroy, Ixion, &c.	Venetia.
Contarini Fleming, &c.	Coningsby.
	Lothair.
Tancred.	Endymion.

Birt.—CASTLE CZVARGAS : a Romance. Being a Plain Story of the Romantic Adventures of Two Brothers, Told by the Younger of Them. Edited by ARCHIBALD BIRT. Crown 8vo., 6s.

'Chola.'—A NEW DIVINITY, AND OTHER STORIES OF HINDU LIFE. By 'CHOLA'. Crown 8vo., 2s. 6d.

Diderot. — RAMEAU'S NEPHEW : a Translation from Diderot's Autographic Text. By SYLVIA MARGARET HILL. Crown 8vo., 3s. 6d.

Dougall. — BEGGARS ALL. By L. DOUGALL. Crown 8vo., 3s. 6d.

Fiction, Humour, &c.—*continued.*

Doyle (A. CONAN).

MICAH CLARKE: a Tale of Monmouth's Rebellion. With 10 Illustrations. Cr. 8vo., 3*s.* 6*d.*

THE CAPTAIN OF THE POLESTAR, and other Tales. Cr. 8vo., 3*s.* 6*d.*

THE REFUGEES: a Tale of the Huguenots. With 25 Illustrations. Crown 8vo., 3*s.* 6*d.*

THE STARK-MUNRO LETTERS. Cr. 8vo., 3*s.* 6*d.*

Farrar (F. W., Dean of Canterbury).

DARKNESS AND DAWN: or, Scenes in the Days of Nero. An Historic Tale. Cr. 8vo., 7*s.* 6*d.*

GATHERING CLOUDS: a Tale of the Days of St. Chrysostom. Crown 8vo., 7*s.* 6*d.*

Fowler (EDITH H.).

THE YOUNG PRETENDERS. A Story of Child Life. With 12 Illustrations by Sir PHILIP BURNE-JONES, Bart. Cr. 8vo., 6*s.*

THE PROFESSOR'S CHILDREN. With 24 Illustrations by ETHEL KATE BURGESS. Crown 8vo., 6*s.*

Francis.—YEOMAN FLEETWOOD. By M. E. FRANCIS, Author of 'In a Northcountry Village,' etc. Cr. 8vo., 6*s.*

Froude.—THE TWO CHIEFS OF DUNBOY: an Irish Romance of the Last Century. By JAMES A. FROUDE. Cr. 8vo., 3*s.* 6*d.*

Gurdon.—MEMORIES AND FANCIES: Suffolk Tales and other Stories; Fairy Legends; Poems; Miscellaneous Articles. By the late LADY CAMILLA GURDON, Author of 'Suffolk Folk-Lore'. Crown 8vo., 5*s.*

Haggard (H. RIDER).

SWALLOW: a Tale of the Great Trek. With 8 Illustrations. Cr. 8vo., 6*s.*

DR. THERNE. Crown 8vo., 3*s.* 5*d.*

HEART OF THE WORLD. With 15 Illustrations. Crown 8vo., 3*s.* 6*d.*

JOAN HASTE. With 20 Illustrations. Cr. 8vo., 3*s.* 6*d.*

Haggard (H. RIDER)—*continued.*

THE PEOPLE OF THE MIST. With 16 Illustrations. Crown 8vo., 3*s.* 6*d.*

MONTEZUMA'S DAUGHTER. With 24 Illustrations. Crown 8vo., 3*s.* 6*d.*

SHE. With 32 Illustrations. Cr. 8vo., 3*s.* 6*d.*

ALLAN QUATERMAIN. With 31 Illustrations. Crown 8vo., 3*s.* 6*d.*

MAIWA'S REVENGE. Crown 8vo., 1*s.* 6*d.*

COLONEL QUARITCH, V.C. With Frontispiece and Vignette. Cr. 8vo., 3*s.* 6*d.*

CLEOPATRA. With 29 Illustrations. Crown 8vo., 3*s.* 6*d.*

BEATRICE. With Frontispiece and Vignette. Crown 8vo., 3*s.* 6*d.*

ERIC BRIGHTEYES. With 51 Illustrations. Cr. 8vo., 3*s.* 6*d.*

NADA THE LILY. With 23 Illustrations. Cr. 8vo., 3*s.* 6*d.*

ALLAN'S WIFE. With 34 Illustrations. Crown 8vo., 3*s.* 6*d.*

THE WITCH'S HEAD. With 16 Illustrations. Crown 8vo., 3*s.* 6*d.*

MR. MEESON'S WILL. With 16 Illustrations. Crown 8vo., 3*s.* 6*d.*

DAWN. With 16 Illustrations. Crown 8vo. 3*s.* 6*d.*

Haggard and Lang.—THE WORLD'S DESIRE. By H. RIDER HAGGARD and ANDREW LANG. With 27 Illustrations. Crown 8vo., 3*s.* 6*d.*

Harte. — IN THE CARQUINEZ WOODS. By BRET HARTE. Cr. 8vo., 3*s.* 6*d.*

Hope.—THE HEART OF PRINCESS OSRA. By ANTHONY HOPE. With 9 Illustrations. Crown 8vo., 6*s.*

Jerome.—SKETCHES IN LAVENDER: Blue and Green. By JEROME K. JEROME. Crown 8vo., 3*s.* 6*d.*

Joyce. — OLD CELTIC ROMANCES. Twelve of the most beautiful of the Ancient Irish Romantic Tales. Translated from the Gaelic. By P. W. JOYCE, LL.D. Crown 8vo., 3*s.* 6*d.*

Fiction, Humour, &c.—*continued.*

Lang.—A MONK OF FIFE: a Story of the Days of Joan of Arc. By ANDREW LANG. With 13 Illustrations by SELWYN IMAGE. Crown 8vo., 3s. 6d.

Levett-Yeats (S.).

THE CHEVALIER D'AURIAC. Crown 8vo., 3s. 6d.

A GALAHAD OF THE CREEKS, and other Stories. Crown 8vo., 6s.

THE HEART OF DENISE, and other Tales. Crown 8vo., 6s.

Lyall (EDNA).

THE AUTOBIOGRAPHY OF A SLANDER. Fcp. 8vo., 1s. sewed.
Presentation Edition. With 20 Illustrations by LANCELOT SPEED. Cr. 8vo., 2s. 6d. net.

THE AUTOBIOGRAPHY OF A TRUTH. Fcp. 8vo., 1s. sewed ; 1s. 6d. cloth.

DOREEN. The Story of a Singer. Cr. 8vo., 6s.

WAYFARING MEN. Crown 8vo., 6s.

HOPE THE HERMIT: a Romance of Borrowdale. Crown 8vo., 6s.

Max Müller. — DEUTSCHE LIEBE (GERMAN LOVE): Fragments from the Papers of an Alien. Collected by F. MAX MÜLLER, Translated from the German by G. A. M. Crown 8vo., 5s.

Melville (G. J. WHYTE).

The Gladiators.	Holmby House.
The Interpreter.	Kate Coventry.
Good for Nothing.	Digby Grand.
The Queen's Maries.	General Bounce.

Cr. 8vo., 1s. 6d. each.

Merriman.—FLOTSAM: a Story of the Indian Mutiny. By HENRY SETON MERRIMAN. Crown 8vo., 3s. 6d.

Morris (WILLIAM).

THE SUNDERING FLOOD. Crown 8vo., 7s. 6d.

THE WATER OF THE WONDROUS ISLES. Crown 8vo., 7s. 6d.

THE WELL AT THE WORLD'S END. 2 vols., 8vo., 28s.

THE STORY OF THE GLITTERING PLAIN, which has been also called The Land of the Living Men, or The Acre of the Undying. Square post 8vo., 5s. net.

Morris (WILLIAM)—*continued.*

THE ROOTS OF THE MOUNTAINS, wherein is told somewhat of the Lives of the Men of Burgdale, their Friends, their Neighbours, their Foemen, and their Fellows-in-Arms. Written in Prose and Verse. Square crown 8vo., 8s.

A TALE OF THE HOUSE OF THE WOLFINGS, and all the Kindreds of the Mark. Written in Prose and Verse. Square crown 8vo., 6s.

A DREAM OF JOHN BALL, AND A KING'S LESSON. 12mo., 1s. 6d.

NEWS FROM NOWHERE ; or, An Epoch of Rest. Being some Chapters from an Utopian Romance. Post 8vo., 1s. 6d.

*** For Mr. William Morris's Poetical Works, see p. 19.

Newman (CARDINAL).

LOSS AND GAIN : The Story of a Convert. Crown 8vo. Cabinet Edition, 6s. ; Popular Edition, 3s. 6d.

CALLISTA: A Tale of the Third Century. Crown 8vo. Cabinet Edition, 6s. ; Popular Edition, 3s. 6d.

Phillipps-Wolley.—SNAP: a Legend of the Lone Mountain. By C. PHILLIPPS-WOLLEY. With 13 Illustrations. Crown 8vo., 3s. 6d.

Raymond (WALTER).

TWO MEN O' MENDIP. Cr. 8vo., 6s.

NO SOUL ABOVE MONEY. Cr. 8vo., 6s.

Reader.—PRIESTESS AND QUEEN: a Tale of the White Race of Mexico ; being the Adventures of Ignigene and her Twenty-six Fair Maidens. By EMILY E. READER. Illustrated by EMILY K. READER. Crown 8vo., 6s.

Sewell (ELIZABETH M.).

A Glimpse of the World.	Amy Herbert.
Laneton Parsonage.	Cleve Hall.
Margaret Percival.	Gertrude.
Katharine Ashton.	Home Life.
The Earl's Daughter.	After Life.
The Experience of Life.	Ursula. Ivors.

Cr. 8vo., 1s. 6d. each, cloth plain. 2s. 6d. each, cloth extra, gilt edges.

Fiction, Humour, &c.—*continued.*

Somerville and Ross.—SOME EX-PERIENCES OF AN IRISH R.M. By E. Œ. SOMERVILLE and MARTIN ROSS. With 31 Illustrations by E. Œ. SOMER-VILLE. Crown 8vo., 6s.

Stebbing.—PROBABLE TALES. Edited by WILLIAM STEBBING Crown 8vo. 4s. 6d.

Stevenson (ROBERT LOUIS).
THE STRANGE CASE OF DR. JEKYLL AND MR. HYDE. Fcp. 8vo., 1s. sewed, 1s. 6d. cloth.
THE STRANGE CASE OF DR. JEKYLL AND MR. HYDE; with Other Fables. Crown 8vo., 3s. 6d.
MORE NEW ARABIAN NIGHTS—THE DYNAMITER. By ROBERT LOUIS STEVENSON and FANNY VAN DE GRIFT STEVENSON. Crown 8vo., 3s. 6d.
THE WRONG BOX. By ROBERT LOUIS STEVENSON and LLOYD OSBOURNE. Crown 8vo., 3s. 6d.

Suttner.—LAY DOWN YOUR ARMS (*Die Waffen Nieder*): The Autobio-graphy of Martha Tilling. By BERTHA VON SUTTNER. Translated by T. HOLMES. Crown 8vo., 1s. 6d.

Taylor. — EARLY ITALIAN LOVE-STORIES. Taken from the Originals by UNA TAYLOR. With 13 Illustrations by HENRY J. FORD. Crown 4to., 15s. net.

Trollope (ANTHONY).
THE WARDEN. Cr. 8vo., 1s. 6d.
BARCHESTER TOWERS. Cr. 8vo., 1s. 6d.

Walford (L. B.).
THE INTRUDERS. Crown 8vo., 6s.
LEDDY MARGET. Crown 8vo., 2s. 6d.
IVA KILDARE: a Matrimonial Problem. Crown 8vo., 6s.
Mr. SMITH: a Part of his Life. Crown 8vo., 2s. 6d.
THE BABY'S GRANDMOTHER. Crown 8vo., 2s. 6d.
COUSINS. Crown 8vo., 2s. 6d.
TROUBLESOME DAUGHTERS. Crown 8vo., 2s. 6d.

Walford (L. B.).—*continued.*
PAULINE. Crown 8vo., 2s. 6d.
DICK NETHERBY. Crown 8vo., 2s. 6d.
THE HISTORY OF A WEEK. Crown 8vo., 2s. 6d.
A STIFF-NECKED GENERATION. Crown 8vo. 2s. 6d.
NAN, and other Stories. Cr. 8vo., 2s. 6d.
THE MISCHIEF OF MONICA. Crown 8vo., 2s. 6d.
THE ONE GOOD GUEST. Cr. 8vo., 2s. 6d.
'PLOUGHED,' and other Stories. Crown 8vo., 2s. 6d.
THE MATCHMAKER. Cr. 8vo., 2s. 6d.

Ward.—ONE POOR SCRUPLE. By Mrs. WILFRID WARD. Crown 8vo., 6s.

Watson.—RACING AND 'CHASING: a Volume of Sporting Stories. By ALFRED E. T. WATSON, Editor of the 'Badminton Magazine'. With 16 Plates and 36 Illustrations in the Text. Crown 8vo., 7s. 6d.

Weyman (STANLEY).
THE HOUSE OF THE WOLF. With Frontispiece and Vignette. Cr. 8vo., 3s. 6d.
A GENTLEMAN OF FRANCE. With Frontispiece and Vignette. Cr. 8vo., 6s.
THE RED COCKADE. With Frontispiece and Vignette. Cr. 8vo., 6s.
SHREWSBURY. With 24 Illustrations by CLAUDE SHEPPERSON. Cr. 8vo., 6s.

Whishaw (FRED.).
A BOYAR OF THE TERRIBLE: a Romance of the Court of Ivan the Cruel, First Tzar of Russia. With 12 Illustrations by H. G. MASSEY, A.R.E. Cr. 8vo., 6s.
A TSAR'S GRATITUDE: a Story of Modern Russia. Cr. 8vo., 6s.

Woods.—WEEPING FERRY, and other Stories. By MARGARET L. WOODS, Author of 'A Village Tragedy'. Crown 8vo., 6s.

Popular Science (Natural History, &c.).

Beddard. — THE STRUCTURE AND CLASSIFICATION OF BIRDS. By FRANK E. BEDDARD, M.A., F.R.S., Prosector and Vice-Secretary of the Zoological Society of London. With 252 Illustra-tions. 8vo., 21s. net.

Butler.—OUR HOUSEHOLD INSECTS. An Account of the Insect-Pests found in Dwelling-Houses. By EDWARD A. BUTLER, B.A., B.Sc. (Lond.). With 113 Illustrations. Crown 8vo., 3s. 6d.

Popular Science (Natural History, &c.).

Furneaux (W.).

THE OUTDOOR WORLD; or, The Young
Collector's Handbook. With 18
Plates (16 of which are coloured)
and 549 Illustrations in the Text.
Crown 8vo., 7s. 6d.

BUTTERFLIES AND MOTHS (British).
With 12 coloured Plates and 241
Illustrations in the Text. Crown 8vo.,
7s. 6d.

LIFE IN PONDS AND STREAMS. With
8 coloured Plates and 331 Illustrations in the Text. Cr. 8vo., 7s. 6d.

Hartwig (Dr. GEORGE).

THE SEA AND ITS LIVING WONDERS.
With 12 Plates and 303 Woodcuts.
8vo., 7s. net.

THE TROPICAL WORLD. With 8 Plates
and 172 Woodcuts. 8vo., 7s. net.

THE POLAR WORLD. With 3 Maps, 8
Plates and 85 Woodcuts. 8vo., 7s. net.

THE SUBTERRANEAN WORLD. With
3 Maps and 80 Woodcuts. 8vo., 7s. net.

THE AERIAL WORLD. With Map, 8
Plates and 60 Woodcuts. 8vo., 7s. net.

HEROES OF THE POLAR WORLD. With
19 Illustrations. Crown 8vo., 2s.

WONDERS OF THE TROPICAL FORESTS.
With 40 Illustrations. Crown 8vo., 2s.

WORKERS UNDER THE GROUND. With
29 Illustrations. Crown 8vo., 2s.

MARVELS OVER OUR HEADS. With 29
Illustrations. Crown 8vo., 2s.

SEA MONSTERS AND SEA BIRDS. With
75 Illustrations. Crown 8vo., 2s. 6d.

DENIZENS OF THE DEEP. With 117
Illustrations. Crown 8vo., 2s. 6d.

VOLCANOES AND EARTHQUAKES. With
30 Illustrations. Crown 8vo., 2s. 6d.

WILD ANIMALS OF THE TROPICS.
With 66 Illustrations. Crown 8vo.,
3s. 6d.

Helmholtz.—POPULAR LECTURES ON
SCIENTIFIC SUBJECTS. By HERMANN
VON HELMHOLTZ. With 68 Woodcuts.
2 vols. Crown 8vo., 3s. 6d. each.

Hudson (W. H.).

BRITISH BIRDS. With a Chapter on
Structure and Classification by FRANK
E. BEDDARD, F.R.S. With 16 Plates
(8 of which are Coloured), and over
100 Illustrations in the Text. Crown
8vo., 7s. 6d.

BIRDS IN LONDON. With 17 Plates
and 15 Illustrations in the Text, by
BRYAN HOOK, A. D. MCCORMICK,
and from Photographs from Nature,
by R. B. LODGE. 8vo., 12s.

Proctor (RICHARD A.).

LIGHT SCIENCE FOR LEISURE HOURS.
Familiar Essays on Scientific Subjects.
3 vols. Crown 8vo., 5s. each. Vol. I.,
Cheap edition, Crown 8vo., 3s. 6d.

ROUGH WAYS MADE SMOOTH. Familiar Essays on Scientific Subjects.
Crown 8vo., 3s. 6d.

PLEASANT WAYS IN SCIENCE.
Crown 8vo., 3s. 6d.

NATURE STUDIES. By R. A. PROCTOR,
GRANT ALLEN, A. WILSON, T. FOS-
TER and E. CLODD. Cr. 8vo., 3s. 6d.

LEISURE READINGS. By R. A. PROC-
TOR, E. CLODD, A. WILSON, T.
FOSTER, and A. C. RANYARD. Cr.
8vo., 3s. 6d.

*** *For Mr. Proctor's other books see
p. 28, and Messrs. Longmans & Co.'s
Catalogue of Scientific Works.*

Stanley.—A FAMILIAR HISTORY OF
BIRDS. By E. STANLEY, D.D., for-
merly Bishop of Norwich. With 160
Illustrations. Crown 8vo., 3s. 6d.

Wood (Rev. J. G.).

HOMES WITHOUT HANDS: a Description of the Habitation of Animals,
classed according to the Principle of
Construction. With 140 Illustrations.
8vo., 7s. net.

INSECTS AT HOME. a Popular Account
of British Insects, their Structure,
Habits and Transformations. With
700 Illustrations. 8vo., 7s. net.

OUT OF DOORS; a Selection of Original Articles on Practical Natural
History. With 11 Illustrations. Cr.
8vo., 3s. 6d.

STRANGE DWELLINGS: a Description
of the Habitations of Animals,
abridged from 'Homes without
Hands'. With 60 Illustrations. Cr.
8vo., 3s. 6d.

PETLAND REVISITED. With 33 Illustrations. Cr. 8vo., 3s. 6d.

BIRD LIFE OF THE BIBLE. With 32
Illustrations. Crown 8vo., 3s. 6d.

WONDERFUL NESTS. With 30 Illustrations. Crown 8vo., 3s. 6d.

HOMES UNDER THE GROUND. With
28 Illustrations. Crown 8vo., 3s. 6d.

WILD ANIMALS OF THE BIBLE. With
29 Illustrations. Crown 8vo., 3s. 6d.

DOMESTIC ANIMALS OF THE BIBLE.
With 23 Illustrations. Cr. 8vo., 3s. 6d.

THE BRANCH BUILDERS. With 28
Illustrations. Crown 8vo., 2s. 6d.

SOCIAL HABITATIONS AND PARASITIC
NESTS. With 18 Illus. Cr. 8vo., 2s.

Works of Reference.

Gwilt.—An Encyclopædia of Architecture. By Joseph Gwilt, F.S.A. Illustrated with more than 1100 Engravings on Wood. Revised (1888), with Alterations and Considerable Additions by Wyatt Papworth. 8vo., £2 12s. 6d.

Maunder (Samuel).

Biographical Treasury. With Supplement brought down to 1889. By Rev. James Wood. Fcp. 8vo., 6s.

Treasury of Geography, Physical, Historical, Descriptive, and Political. With 7 Maps and 16 Plates. Fcp. 8vo., 6s.

The Treasury of Bible Knowledge. By the Rev. J. Ayre, M.A. With 5 Maps, 15 Plates, and 300 Woodcuts. Fcp. 8vo., 6s.

Treasury of Knowledge and Library of Reference. Fcp. 8vo., 6s.

Historical Treasury : Fcp. 8vo., 6s.

Maunder (Samuel)—*continued.*

Scientific and Literary Treasury. Fcp. 8vo., 6s.

The Treasury of Botany. Edited by J. Lindley, F.R.S., and T. Moore, F.L.S. With 274 Woodcuts and 20 Steel Plates. 2 vols. Fcp. 8vo., 12s.

Roget.—Thesaurus of English Words and Phrases. Classified and Arranged so as to Facilitate the Expression of Ideas and assist in Literary Composition. By Peter Mark Roget, M.D., F.R.S. Recomposed throughout, enlarged and improved, partly from the Author's Notes and with a full Index, by the Author's Son, John Lewis Roget. Crown 8vo., 10s. 6d.

Willich.—Popular Tables for giving information for ascertaining the value of Lifehold, Leasehold, and Church Property, the Public Funds, &c. By Charles M. Willich. Edited by H. Bence Jones. Crown 8vo., 10s. 6d.

Children's Books.

Buckland.—Two Little Runaways. Adapted from the French of Louis Desnoyers. By James Buckland. With 110 Illustrations by Cecil Aldin. Crown 8vo., 6s.

Crake (Rev. A. D.).

Edwy the Fair; or, the First Chronicle of Æscendune. Crown 8vo., 2s.6d.

Alfgar the Dane: or, the Second Chronicle of Æscendune. Cr. 8vo., 2s. 6d.

The Rival Heirs: being the Third and Last Chronicle of Æscendune. Crown 8vo., 2s. 6d.

The House of Walderne. A Tale of the Cloister and the Forest in the Days of the Barons' Wars. Crown 8vo., 2s. 6d.

Brian Fitz-Count. A Story of Wallingford Castle and Dorchester Abbey. Crown 8vo., 2s. 6d.

Henty (G. A.).—Edited by.

Yule Logs : A Story-Book for Boys. With 61 Illustrations. Crown 8vo., 6s.

Yule Tide Yarns. With 45 Illustrations. Crown 8vo., 6s.

Lang (Andrew)—Edited by.

The Blue Fairy Book. With 138 Illustrations. Crown 8vo., 6s.

The Red Fairy Book. With 100 Illustrations. Crown 8vo., 6s.

The Green Fairy Book. With 99 Illustrations. Crown 8vo., 6s.

The Yellow Fairy Book. With 104 Illustrations. Crown 8vo., 6s.

The Pink Fairy Book. With 67 Illustrations. Crown 8vo., 6s.

The Blue Poetry Book. With 100 Illustrations. Crown 8vo., 6s.

The Blue Poetry Book. School Edition, without Illustrations. Fcp. 8vo., 2s. 6d.

The True Story Book. With 66 Illustrations. Crown 8vo., 6s.

The Red True Story Book. With 100 Illustrations. Crown 8vo., 6s.

The Animal Story Book. With 67 Illustrations. Crown 8vo., 6s.

The Red Book of Animal Stories. With 65 Illustrations. Cr. 8vo., 6s.

The Arabian Nights Entertainments. With 66 Illustrations. Crown 8vo., 6s.

Children's Books—*continued.*

Meade (L. T.).

DADDY'S BOY. With 8 Illustrations. Crown 8vo., 3s. 6d.

DEB AND THE DUCHESS. With 7 Illustrations. Crown 8vo., 3s. 6d.

THE BERESFORD PRIZE. With 7 Illustions. Crown 8vo., 3s. 6d.

THE HOUSE OF SURPRISES. With 6 Illustrations. Crown 8vo., 3s. 6d.

Praeger (ROSAMOND).

THE ADVENTURES OF THE THREE BOLD BABES: Hector, Honoria and Alisander. A Story in Pictures. With 24 Coloured Plates and 24 Outline Pictures. Oblong 4to., 3s. 6d.

THE FURTHER DOINGS OF THE THREE BOLD BABES. With 24 Coloured Plates and 24 Outline Pictures. Oblong 4to., 3s. 6d.

Stevenson.—A CHILD'S GARDEN OF VERSES. By ROBERT LOUIS STEVENSON. fcp. 8vo., 5s.

Upton (FLORENCE K., and BERTHA).

THE ADVENTURES OF TWO DUTCH DOLLS AND A 'GOLLIWOGG'. With 31 Coloured Plates and numerous Illustrations in the Text. Oblong 4to., 6s.

THE GOLLIWOGG'S BICYCLE CLUB. With 31 Coloured Plates and numerous Illustrations in the Text. Oblong 4to., 6s.

THE GOLLIWOGG AT THE SEASIDE. With 31 Coloured Plates and numerous Illustrations in the Text. Oblong 4to., 6s.

THE GOLLIWOGG IN WAR. With 31 Coloured Plates. Oblong 4to., 6s.

THE VEGE-MEN'S REVENGE. With 31 Coloured Plates and numerous Illustrations in the Text. Oblong 4to., 6s.

The Silver Library.

CROWN 8vo. 3s. 6d. EACH VOLUME.

Arnold's (Sir Edwin) Seas and Lands. With 71 Illustrations. 3s. 6d.

Bagehot's (W.) Biographical Studies. 3s. 6d.

Bagehot's (W.) Economic Studies. 3s. 6d.

Bagehot's (W.) Literary Studies. With Portrait. 3 vols. 3s. 6d. each.

Baker's (Sir S. W.) Eight Years in Ceylon. With 6 Illustrations. 3s. 6d.

Baker's (Sir S. W.) Rifle and Hound in Ceylon. With 6 Illustrations. 3s. 6d.

Baring-Gould's (Rev. S.) Curious Myths of the Middle Ages. 3s. 6d.

Baring-Gould's (Rev. S.) Origin and Development of Religious Belief. 2 vols. 3s. 6d. each.

Becker's (W. A.) Gallus: or, Roman Scenes in the Time of Augustus. With 26 Illustrations. 3s. 6d.

Becker's (W. A.) Charicles: or, Illustrations of the Private Life of the Ancient Greeks. With 26 Illustrations. 3s. 6d.

Bent's (J. T.) The Ruined Cities of Mashonaland. With 117 Illustrations. 3s. 6d.

Brassey's (Lady) A Voyage in the 'Sunbeam'. With 66 Illustrations. 3s. 6d.

Churchill's (W. S.) The Story of the Malakand Field Force, 1897. With 6 Maps and Plans. 3s. 6d.

Clodd's (E.) Story of Creation: a Plain Account of Evolution. With 77 Illustrations. 3s. 6d.

Conybeare (Rev. W. J.) and Howson's (Very Rev. J. S.) Life and Epistles of St. Paul. With 46 Illustrations. 3s. 6d.

Dougall's (L.) Beggars All; a Novel. 3s. 6d.

Doyle's (A. Conan) Micah Clarke. A Tale of Monmouth's Rebellion. With 10 Illustrations. 3s. 6d.

Doyle's (A. Conan) The Captain of the Polestar, and other Tales. 3s. 6d.

Doyle's (A. Conan) The Refugees: A Tale of the Huguenots. With 25 Illustrations. 3s. 6d.

Doyle's (A. Conan) The Stark Munro Letters. 3s. 6d.

Froude's (J. A.) The History of England, from the Fall of Wolsey to the Defeat of the Spanish Armada. 12 vols. 3s. 6d. each.

The Silver Library—*continued.*

Froude's (J. A.) The English in Ireland. 3 vols. 10s. 6d.

Froude's (J. A.) The Divorce of Catherine of Aragon. 3s. 6d.

Froude's (J. A.) The Spanish Story of the Armada, and other Essays. 3s. 6d.

Froude's (J. A.) Short Studies on Great Subjects. 4 vols. 3s. 6d. each.

Froude's (J. A.) Oceana, or England and Her Colonies. With 9 Illustrations. 3s. 6d.

Froude's (J. A.) The Council of Trent. 3s. 6d.

Froude's (J. A.) The Life and Letters of Erasmus. 3s. 6d.

Froude's (J. A.) Thomas Carlyle: a History of his Life. 1795-1835. 2 vols. 7s. 1834-1881. 2 vols. 7s.

Froude's (J. A.) Cæsar: a Sketch. 3s. 6d.

Froude's (J. A.) The Two Chiefs of Dunboy: an Irish Romance of the Last Century. 3s. 6d.

Gleig's (Rev. G. R.) Life of the Duke of Wellington. With Portrait. 3s. 6d.

Greville's (C. C. F.) Journal of the Reigns of King George IV., King William IV., and Queen Victoria. 8 vols, 3s. 6d. each.

Haggard's (H. R.) She: A History of Adventure. With 32 Illustrations. 3s. 6d.

Haggard's (H. R.) Allan Quatermain. With 20 Illustrations. 3s. 6d.

Haggard's (H. R.) Colonel Quaritch, V.C.: a Tale of Country Life. With Frontispiece and Vignette. 3s. 6d.

Haggard's (H. R.) Cleopatra. With 29 Illustrations. 3s. 6d.

Haggard's (H. R.) Eric Brighteyes. With 51 Illustrations. 3s. 6d.

Haggard's (H. R.) Beatrice. With Frontispiece and Vignette. 3s. 6d.

Haggard's (H. R.) Allan's Wife. With 34 Illustrations. 3s. 6d.

Haggard's (H. R.) Heart of the World. With 15 Illustrations. 3s. 6d.

Haggard's (H. R.) Montezuma's Daughter. With 25 Illustrations. 3s. 6d.

Haggard's (H. R.) The Witch's Head. With 16 Illustrations. 3s. 6d.

Haggard's (H. R.) Mr. Meeson's Will. With 16 Illustrations. 3s. 6d.

Haggard's (H. R.) Nada the Lily. With 23 Illustrations. 3s. 6d.

Haggard's (H. R.) Dawn. With 16 Illustrations. 3s. 6d.

Haggard's (H. R.) The People of the Mist. With 16 Illustrations. 3s. 6d.

Haggard's (H. R.) Joan Haste. With 20 Illustrations. 3s. 6d.

Haggard (H. R.) and Lang's (A.) The World's Desire. With 27 Illus. 3s. 6d.

Harte's (Bret) In the Carquinez Woods, and other Stories. 3s. 6d.

Helmholtz's (Hermann von) Popular Lectures on Scientific Subjects. With 68 Illustrations. 2 vols. 3s. 6d. each.

Hornung's (E. W.) The Unbidden Guest. 3s. 6d.

Howitt's (W.) Visits to Remarkable Places. With 80 Illustrations. 3s. 6d.

Jefferies' (R.) The Story of My Heart: My Autobiography. With Portrait. 3s. 6d.

Jefferies' (R.) Field and Hedgerow. With Portrait. 3s. 6d.

Jefferies' (R.) Red Deer. 17 Illus. 3s. 6d.

Jefferies' (R.) Wood Magic: a Fable. With Frontispiece and Vignette by E. V. B. 3s. 6d.

Jefferies' (R.) The Toilers of the Field. With Portrait from the Bust in Salisbury Cathedral. 3s. 6d.

Kaye (Sir J.) and Malleson's (Colonel) History of the Indian Mutiny of 1857-8. 6 vols. 3s. 6d. each.

Knight's (E. F.) The Cruise of the 'Alerte': the Narrative of a Search for Treasure on the Desert Island of Trinidad. With 2 Maps and 23 Illustrations. 3s. 6d.

Knight's (E. F.) Where Three Empires Meet: a Narrative of Recent Travel in Kashmir, Western Tibet, Baltistan, Gilgit. With a Map and 54 Illustrations. 3s. 6d

Knight's (E. F.) The 'Falcon' on the Baltic: a Coasting Voyage from Hammersmith to Copenhagen in a Three-Ton Yacht. With Map and 11 Illustrations. 3s. 6d.

Köstlin's (J.) Life of Luther. With 62 Illustrations and 4 Facsimiles of MSS. 3s. 6d.

Lang's (A.) Angling Sketches. With 20 Illustrations. 3s. 6d.

Lang's (A.) Custom and Myth: Studies of Early Usage and Belief. 3s. 6d.

Lang's (A.) Cock Lane and Common-Sense. 3s. 6d.

Lang's (A.) The Book of Dreams and Ghosts. 3s. 6d.

Lang's (A.) A Monk of Fife: a Story of the Days of Joan of Arc. With 13 Illustrations. 3s. 6d.

Lang's (A.) Myth, Ritual, and Religion. 2 vols. 7s.

The Silver Library—*continued.*

Lees (J. A.) and Clutterbuck's (W.J.)B.C. 1887, A Ramble in British Columbia. With Maps and 75 Illustrations. 3*s. 6d.*

Levett-Yeats' (S.) The Chevalier D'Auriac. 3*s. 6d.*

Macaulay's (Lord) Complete Works. 'Albany' Edition. With 12 Portraits. 12 vols. 3*s. 6d.* each.

Macaulay's (Lord) Essays and Lays of Ancient Rome, etc. With Portrait and 4 Illustrations to the 'Lays'. 3*s. 6d.*

Macleod's (H. D.) Elements of Banking. 3*s. 6d.*

Marbot's (Baron de) Memoirs. Translated. 2 vols. 7*s.*

Marshman's (J. C.) Memoirs of Sir Henry Havelock. 3*s. 6d.*

Merivale's (Dean) History of the Romans under the Empire. 8 vols. 3*s. 6d.* ea.

Merriman's (H. S.) Flotsam : a Tale of the Indian Mutiny. 3*s. 6d.*

Mill's (J. S.) Political Economy. 3*s. 6d.*

Mill's (J. S.) System of Logic. 3*s. 6d.*

Milner's (Geo.) Country Pleasures : the Chronicle of a Year chiefly in a Garden. 3*s. 6d.*

Nansen's (F.) The First Crossing of Greenland. With 142 Illustrations and a Map. 3*s. 6d.*

Phillipps-Wolley's (C.) Snap : a Legend of the Lone Mountain. With 13 Illustrations. 3*s. 6d.*

Proctor's (R. A.) The Orbs Around Us. 3*s. 6d.*

Proctor's (R. A.) The Expanse of Heaven. 3*s. 6d.*

Proctor's (R. A.) Light Science for Leisure Hours. First Series. 3*s. 6d.*

Proctor's (R. A.) The Moon. 3*s. 6d.*

Proctor's (R. A.) Other Worlds than Ours. 3*s. 6d.*

Proctor's (R. A.) Our Place among Infinities : a Series of Essays contrasting our Little Abode in Space and Time with the Infinities around us. 3*s. 6d.*

Proctor's (R. A.) Other Suns than Ours. 3*s. 6d.*

Proctor's (R. A.) Rough Ways made Smooth. 3*s. 6d.*

Proctor's (R. A.) Pleasant Ways in Science. 3*s. 6d.*

Proctor's (R. A.) Myths and Marvels of Astronomy. 3*s. 6d.*

Proctor's (R. A.) Nature Studies. 3*s. 6d.*

Proctor's (R. A.) Leisure Readings. By R. A. PROCTOR, EDWARD CLODD, ANDREW WILSON, THOMAS FOSTER, and A. C. RANYARD. With Illustrations. 3*s. 6d.*

Rossetti's (Maria F.) A Shadow of Dante. 3*s. 6d.*

Smith's (R. Bosworth) Carthage and the Carthaginians. With Maps, Plans, &c. 3*s. 6d.*

Stanley's (Bishop) Familiar History of Birds. With 160 Illustrations. 3*s. 6d.*

Stephen's (L.) The Playground of Europe (The Alps). With 4 Illustrations. 3*s. 6d.*

Stevenson's (R. L.) The Strange Case of Dr. Jekyll and Mr. Hyde; with other Fables. 3*s. 6d.*

Stevenson (R. L.) and Osbourne's (Ll.) The Wrong Box. 3*s. 6d.*

Stevenson (Robt. Louis) and Stevenson's (Fanny van de Grift) More New Arabian Nights. — The Dynamiter. 3*s. 6d.*

Trevelyan's (Sir G. O.) The Early History of Charles James Fox. 3*s. 6d.*

Weyman's (Stanley J.) The House of the Wolf : a Romance. 3*s. 6d.*

Wood's (Rev. J. G.) Petland Revisited. With 33 Illustrations. 3*s. 6d.*

Wood's (Rev. J. G.) Strange Dwellings. With 60 Illustrations. 3*s. 6d.*

Wood's (Rev. J. G.) Out of Doors. With 11 Illustrations. 3*s. 6d.*

Cookery, Domestic Management, &c.

Acton.—MODERN COOKERY. By ELIZA ACTON. With 150 Woodcuts. Fcp. 8vo., 4*s. 6d.*

Ashby.—HEALTH IN THE NURSERY. By HENRY ASHBY, M.D., F.R.C.P., Physician to the Manchester Children's Hospital, and Lecturer on the Diseases of Children at the Owens College. With 25 Illustrations. Cr. 8vo., 3*s. 6d.*

Buckton.—COMFORT AND CLEANLINESS: The Servant and Mistress Question. By Mrs. CATHERINE M. BUCKTON. With 14 Illustrations. Crown 8vo., 2*s.*

Bull (THOMAS, M.D.).

HINTS TO MOTHERS ON THE MANAGEMENT OF THEIR HEALTH DURING THE PERIOD OF PREGNANCY. Fcp. 8vo., 1*s. 6d.*

Cookery, Domestic Management, &c.—*continued.*

Bull (THOMAS, M.D.)—*continued.*
THE MATERNAL MANAGEMENT OF CHILDREN IN HEALTH AND DISEASE. Fcp. 8vo., 1s. 6d.

De Salis (Mrs.).
CAKES AND CONFECTIONS À LA MODE. Fcp. 8vo., 1s. 6d.
DOGS: a Manual for Amateurs. Fcp. 8vo., 1s. 6d.
DRESSED GAME AND POULTRY À LA MODE. Fcp. 8vo., 1s. 6d.
DRESSED VEGETABLES À LA MODE. Fcp. 8vo., 1s. 6d.
DRINKS À LA MODE. Fcp. 8vo., 1s. 6d.
ENTRÉES À LA MODE. Fcp. 8vo., 1s. 6d.
FLORAL DECORATIONS. Fcp. 8vo., 1s. 6d.
GARDENING À LA MODE. Fcp. 8vo.
Part I. Vegetables. 1s. 6d.
Part II. Fruits. 1s. 6d.
NATIONAL VIANDS À LA MODE. Fcp. 8vo., 1s. 6d.
NEW-LAID EGGS. Fcp. 8vo., 1s. 6d.
OYSTERS À LA MODE. Fcp. 8vo., 1s. 6d.
SOUPS AND DRESSED FISH À LA MODE. Fcp. 8vo., 1s. 6d.
SAVOURIES À LA MODE. Fcp. 8vo., 1s. 6d.
PUDDINGS AND PASTRY À LA MODE. Fcp. 8vo., 1s. 6d.

De Salis (Mrs.)—*continued.*
SWEETS AND SUPPER DISHES À LA MODE. Fcp. 8vo., 1s. 6d.
TEMPTING DISHES FOR SMALL INCOMES. Fcp. 8vo., 1s. 6d.
WRINKLES AND NOTIONS FOR EVERY HOUSEHOLD. Cr. 8vo., 1s. 6d.

Lear.—MAIGRE COOKERY. By H. L. SIDNEY LEAR. 16mo., 2s.

Mann.—MANUAL OF THE PRINCIPLES OF PRACTICAL COOKERY. By E. E. MANN. Crown 8vo., 1s.

Poole.—COOKERY FOR THE DIABETIC. By W. H. and Mrs. POOLE. With Preface by Dr. PAVY. Fcp. 8vo., 2s. 6d.

Walker (JANE H.).
A BOOK FOR EVERY WOMAN.
Part I. The Management of Children in Health and out of Health. Cr. 8vo., 2s. 6d.
Part II. Woman in Health and out of Health. Crown 8vo, 2s. 6d.
A HANDBOOK FOR MOTHERS: being Simple Hints to Women on the Management of their Health during Pregnancy and Confinement, together with Plain Directions as to the Care of Infants. Cr. 8vo., 2s. 6d.

Miscellaneous and Critical Works.

Armstrong.—ESSAYS AND SKETCHES. By EDMUND J. ARMSTRONG. Fcp. 8vo., 5s.

Bagehot.—LITERARY STUDIES. By WALTER BAGEHOT. With Portrait. 3 vols. Crown 8vo., 3s. 6d. each.

Baring-Gould.—CURIOUS MYTHS OF THE MIDDLE AGES. By Rev. S. BARING-GOULD. Crown 8vo., 3s. 6d.

Baynes.—SHAKESPEARE STUDIES, AND OTHER ESSAYS. By the late THOMAS SPENCER BAYNES, LL.B., LL.D. With a Biographical Preface by Prof. LEWIS CAMPBELL. Crown 8vo., 7s. 6d.

Boyd (A. K. H.) ('A.K.H.B.').
And see MISCELLANEOUS THEOLOGICAL WORKS, p. 32.
AUTUMN HOLIDAYS OF A COUNTRY PARSON. Crown 8vo., 3s. 6d.
COMMONPLACE PHILOSOPHER. Crown 8vo., 3s. 6d.
CRITICAL ESSAYS OF A COUNTRY PARSON. Crown 8vo., 3s. 6d.
EAST COAST DAYS AND MEMORIES. Crown 8vo., 3s. 6d.
LANDSCAPES, CHURCHES AND MORALITIES. Crown 8vo., 3s. 6d.
LEISURE HOURS IN TOWN. Crown 8vo., 3s. 6d.

Boyd (A. K. H.) ('A.K.H.B.')—*continued.*
LESSONS OF MIDDLE AGE. Cr. 8vo., 3s. 6d.
OUR LITTLE LIFE. Two Series. Cr. 8vo., 3s. 6d. each.
OUR HOMELY COMEDY: AND TRAGEDY. Crown 8vo., 3s. 6d.
RECREATIONS OF A COUNTRY PARSON. Three Series. Cr. 8vo., 3s. 6d. each.

Butler (SAMUEL).
EREWHON. Cr. 8vo., 5s.
THE FAIR HAVEN. A Work in Defence of the Miraculous Element in our Lord's Ministry. Cr. 8vo., 7s. 6d.
LIFE AND HABIT. An Essay after a Completer View of Evolution. Cr. 8vo., 7s. 6d.
EVOLUTION, OLD AND NEW. Cr. 8vo., 10s. 6d.
ALPS AND SANCTUARIES OF PIEDMONT AND CANTON TICINO. Illustrated. Pott 4to., 10s. 6d.
LUCK, OR CUNNING, AS THE MAIN MEANS OF ORGANIC MODIFICATION? Cr. 8vo., 7s. 6d.
EX VOTO. An Account of the Sacro Monte or New Jerusalem at Varallo-Sesia. Crown 8vo., 10s. 6d.

Miscellaneous and Critical Works —*continued.*

Butler (SAMUEL)—*continued.*

SELECTIONS FROM WORKS, with Remarks on Mr. G. J. Romanes' 'Mental Evolution in Animals,' and a Psalm of Montreal. Crown 8vo., 7s. 6d.

THE AUTHORESS OF THE ODYSSEY, WHERE AND WHEN SHE WROTE, WHO SHE WAS, THE USE SHE MADE OF THE ILIAD, AND HOW THE POEM GREW UNDER HER HANDS. With 14 Illustrations. 8vo., 10s. 6d.

THE ILIAD OF HOMER. Rendered into English Prose for the use of those who cannot read the original. Crown 8vo., 7s. 6d.

SHAKESPEARE'S SONNETS. Reconsidered, and in part Rearranged, with Introductory Chapters and a Reprint of the Original 1609 Edition. 8vo.

Calder.—ACCIDENT IN FACTORIES: its Distribution, Causation, Compensation, and Prevention. A Practical Guide to the Law and to the Safe-Guarding, Safe-Working, and Safe-Construction of Factory Machinery, Plant, and Premises. With 20 Tables and 124 Illustrations. By JOHN CALDER.

CHARITIES REGISTER, THE ANNUAL, AND DIGEST: being a Classified Register of Charities in or available in the Metropolis. With an Introduction by C. S. LOCH, Secretary to the Council of the Charity Organisation Society, London. 8vo., 4s.

Comparetti. — THE TRADITIONAL POETRY OF THE FINNS. By DOMENICO COMPARETTI. Translated by ISABELLA M. ANDERTON. With Introduction by ANDREW LANG. 8vo., 16s.

Evans.—THE ANCIENT STONE IMPLEMENTS, WEAPONS, AND ORNAMENTS OF GREAT BRITAIN. By Sir JOHN EVANS, K.C.B., D.C.L., LL.D., F.R.S., etc. With 537 Illustrations. Medium 8vo., 28s.

Haggard.—A FARMERS' YEAR: being his Commonplace Book for 1898. By H. RIDER HAGGARD. With 36 Illustrations by C. LEON LITTLE. Crown 8vo., 7s. 6d. net.

Hamlin.—A TEXT-BOOK OF THE HISTORY OF ARCHITECTURE. By A. D. F. HAMLIN, A.M. With 229 Illustrations. Crown 8vo., 7s. 6d.

Haweis.—MUSIC AND MORALS. By the Rev. H. R. HAWEIS. With Portrait of the Author, and numerous Illustrations, Facsimiles and Diagrams. Cr. 8vo., 7s. 6d.

Hodgson. — OUTCAST ESSAYS AND VERSE TRANSLATIONS. By SHADWORTH H. HODGSON, LL.D. Crown 8vo., 8s. 6d.

Hoenig.—INQUIRIES CONCERNING THE TACTICS OF THE FUTURE. Fourth Edition, 1894, of the 'Two Brigades'. By FRITZ HOENIG. With 1 Sketch in the Text and 5 Maps. Translated by Captain H. M. BOWER. 8vo., 15s. net.

Hullah.—THE HISTORY OF MODERN MUSIC. By JOHN HULLAH. 8vo., 8s. 6d

Jefferies (RICHARD).

FIELD AND HEDGEROW. With Portrait. Crown 8vo., 3s. 6d.

THE STORY OF MY HEART: my Autobiography. With Portrait and New Preface by C. J. LONGMAN. Crown 8vo., 3s. 6d.

RED DEER. With 17 Illustrations. Crown 8vo., 3s. 6d.

THE TOILERS OF THE FIELD. With Portrait from the Bust in Salisbury Cathedral. Crown 8vo., 3s. 6d.

WOOD MAGIC: a Fable. With Frontispiece and Vignette by E. V. B. Cr. 8vo., 3s. 6d.

Jekyll.—WOOD AND GARDEN: Notes and Thoughts, Practical and Critical, of a Working Amateur. By GERTRUDE JEKYLL. 71 Illustrations from Photographs by the Author. 8vo., 10s. 6d. net.

Johnson.—THE PATENTEE'S MANUAL: a Treatise on the Law and Practice of Letters Patent. By J. & J. H. JOHNSON, Patent Agents, &c. 8vo., 10s. 6d.

Joyce.—THE ORIGIN AND HISTORY OF IRISH NAMES OF PLACES. By P. W. JOYCE, LL.D. 2 vols. Crown 8vo., 5s. each.

Kingsley.—A HISTORY OF FRENCH ART, 1100-1899. By ROSE C. KINGSLEY. 8vo., 12s. 6d. net.

Lang (ANDREW).

LETTERS TO DEAD AUTHORS. Fcp. 8vo., 2s. 6d. net.

BOOKS AND BOOKMEN. With 2 Coloured Plates and 17 Illustrations. Fcp. 8vo., 2s. 6d. net.

OLD FRIENDS. Fcp. 8vo., 2s. 6d. net.

LETTERS ON LITERATURE. Fcp. 8vo., 2s. 6d. net.

ESSAYS IN LITTLE. With Portrait of the Author. Crown 8vo., 2s. 6d.

COCK LANE AND COMMON-SENSE. Crown 8vo., 3s. 6d.

THE BOOK OF DREAMS AND GHOSTS. Crown 8vo., 6s.

Macfarren.—LECTURES ON HARMONY. By Sir G. A. MACFARREN. 8vo., 12s.

Miscellaneous and Critical Works—*continued.*

Marquand and Frothingham.—A TEXT-BOOK OF THE HISTORY OF SCULPTURE. By ALLAN MARQUAND, Ph.D., and ARTHUR L. FROTHINGHAM, Junr., Ph.D., Professors of Archæology and the History of Art in Princetown University. With 113 Illustrations. Crown 8vo., 6s.

Max Müller (The Right Hon. F.).
INDIA: WHAT CAN IT TEACH US? Cr. 8vo., 5s.
CHIPS FROM A GERMAN WORKSHOP.
Vol. I. Recent Essays and Addresses. Cr. 8vo., 5s.
Vol. II. Biographical Essays. Cr. 8vo., 5s.
Vol. III. Essays on Language and Literature. Cr. 8vo., 5s.
Vol. IV. Essays on Mythology and Folk Lore. Crown 8vo., 5s.
CONTRIBUTIONS TO THE SCIENCE OF MYTHOLOGY. 2 vols. 8vo., 32s.

Milner. — COUNTRY PLEASURES: the Chronicle of a Year chiefly in a Garden. By GEORGE MILNER. Cr. 8vo., 3s. 6d.

Morris (WILLIAM).
SIGNS OF CHANGE. Seven Lectures delivered on various occasions. Post 8vo., 4s. 6d.
HOPES AND FEARS FOR ART. Five Lectures delivered in Birmingham, London, etc., 1878-1881. Cr. 8vo., 4s. 6d.
AN ADDRESS DELIVERED AT THE DISTRIBUTION OF PRIZES TO STUDENTS OF THE BIRMINGHAM MUNICIPAL SCHOOL OF ART ON 21ST FEBRUARY, 1894. 8vo., 2s. 6d. net.
ART AND THE BEAUTY OF THE EARTH: a Lecture delivered at Burslem Town Hall, on October 13, 1881. 8vo., 2s. 6d. net.
ARTS AND CRAFTS ESSAYS. By Members of the Arts and Crafts Exhibition Society. With a Preface by WILLIAM MORRIS. Crown 8vo., 2s. 6d. net.
SOME HINTS ON PATTERN-DESIGNING: a Lecture delivered by WILLIAM MORRIS at the Working Men's College, London, on December 10, 1881. 8vo., 2s. 6d. net.

Pollock.—JANE AUSTEN: her Contemporaries and Herself. An Essay in Criticism. By WALTER HERRIES POLLOCK. Crown 8vo.

Poore(GEORGE VIVIAN, M.D., F.R.C.P.).
ESSAYS ON RURAL HYGIENE. With 13 Illustrations. Crown 8vo., 6s. 6d.
THE DWELLING HOUSE. With 36 Illustrations. Crown 8vo., 3s. 6d.

Richmond. — BOYHOOD: a Plea for Continuity in Education. By ENNIS RICHMOND. Crown 8vo., 2s. 6d.

Richter. — LECTURES ON THE NATIONAL GALLERY. By J. P. RICHTER. With 20 Plates and 7 Illustrations in the Text. Crown 4to., 9s.

Rossetti.—A SHADOW OF DANTE: being an Essay towards studying Himself, his World, and his Pilgrimage. By MARIA FRANCESCA ROSSETTI. With Frontispiece by DANTE GABRIEL ROSSETTI. Crown 8vo., 3s. 6d.

Shadwell. — THE LONDON WATER SUPPLY. BY ARTHUR SHADWELL, M.A., M.B.Oxon., Member of the Royal College of Physicians. Crown 8vo., 5s.

Soulsby (LUCY H. M.).
STRAY THOUGHTS ON READING. Small 8vo., 2s. 6d. net.
STRAY THOUGHTS FOR GIRLS. 16mo., 1s. 6d. net.
STRAY THOUGHTS FOR MOTHERS AND TEACHERS. Fcp. 8vo., 2s. 6d. net.
STRAY THOUGHTS FOR INVALIDS. 16mo., 2s. net.

Southey.—THE CORRESPONDENCE OF ROBERT SOUTHEY WITH CAROLINE BOWLES. Edited, with an Introduction, by EDWARD DOWDEN, LL.D. 8vo., 14s.

Stevens.—ON THE STOWAGE OF SHIPS AND THEIR CARGOES. With Information regarding Freights, Charter-Parties, &c. By ROBERT WHITE STEVENS, Associate-Member of the Institute of Naval Architects. 8vo., 21s.

Turner and Sutherland. — THE DEVELOPMENT OF AUSTRALIAN LITERATURE. By HENRY GYLES TURNER and ALEXANDER SUTHERLAND. With Portraits and Illustrations. Cr. 8vo., 5s.

Van Dyke.—A TEXT-BOOK ON THE HISTORY OF PAINTING. By JOHN C. VAN DYKE, Professor of the History of Art in Rutgers College, U.S. With 110 Illustrations. Crown 8vo., 6s.

Warwick.—PROGRESS IN WOMEN'S EDUCATION IN THE BRITISH EMPIRE: being the Report of Conferences and a Congress held in connection with the Educational Section, Victorian Era Exhibition. Edited by the COUNTESS OF WARWICK. Crown 8vo., 6s.

White.—AN EXAMINATION OF THE CHARGE OF APOSTACY AGAINST WORDSWORTH. By W. HALE WHITE, Editor of the 'Description of the Wordsworth and Coleridge MSS. in the Possession of Mr. T. Norton Longman'. Crown 8vo., 3s. 6d.

Willard. — HISTORY OF MODERN ITALIAN ART. By ASHTON ROLLINS WILLARD. With Photogravure Frontispiece and 28 Full-page Illustrations. 8vo., 18s. net.

Miscellaneous Theological Works.

. *For Church of England and Roman Catholic Works see* MESSRS. LONGMANS & CO.'S
Special Catalogues.

Balfour.—THE FOUNDATIONS OF BE-
LIEF : being Notes Introductory to the
Study of Theology. By the Right Hon.
ARTHUR J. BALFOUR, M.P. 8vo., 12s. 6d.

Boyd (A. K. H.) ('A.K.H.B.').
OCCASIONAL AND IMMEMORIAL DAYS :
Discourses. Crown 8vo., 7s. 6d.
COUNSEL AND COMFORT FROM A CITY
PULPIT. Crown 8vo., 3s. 6d.
SUNDAY AFTERNOONS IN THE PARISH
CHURCH OF A SCOTTISH UNIVERSITY
CITY. Crown 8vo., 3s. 6d.
CHANGED ASPECTS OF UNCHANGED
TRUTHS. Crown 8vo., 3s. 6d.
GRAVER THOUGHTS OF A COUNTRY
PARSON. Three Series. Crown 8vo.,
3s. 6d. each.
PRESENT DAY THOUGHTS. Crown 8vo.,
3s. 6d.
SEASIDE MUSINGS. Cr. 8vo., 3s. 6d.
'TO MEET THE DAY' through the
Christian Year ; being a Text of Scrip-
ture, with an Original Meditation and
a Short Selection in Verse for Every
Day. Crown 8vo., 4s. 6d.

Campbell. — RELIGION IN GREEK
LITERATURE. By the Rev. LEWIS
CAMPBELL, M.A., LL.D., Emeritus
Professor of Greek, University of St.
Andrews. 8vo., 15s.

Davidson.—THEISM, as Grounded in
Human Nature, Historically and Critic-
ally Handled. Being the Burnett
Lectures for 1892 and 1893, delivered at
Aberdeen. By W. L. DAVIDSON, M.A.,
LL.D. 8vo., 15s.

Gibson.—THE ABBÉ DE LAMENNAIS
AND THE LIBERAL CATHOLIC MOVE-
MENT IN FRANCE. By the HON. W.
GIBSON. With Portrait. 8vo., 12s. 6d.

Lang (ANDREW).
THE MAKING OF RELIGION. 8vo., 12s.
MODERN MYTHOLOGY : a Reply to Pro-
fessor Max Müller. 8vo., 9s.

MacDonald (GEORGE).
UNSPOKEN SERMONS. Three Series.
Crown 8vo., 3s. 6d. each.
THE MIRACLES OF OUR LORD. Crown
8vo., 3s. 6d.

Martineau (JAMES).
HOURS OF THOUGHT ON SACRED
THINGS : Sermons. 2 Vols. Crown
8vo. 3s. 6d. each.
ENDEAVOURS AFTER THE CHRISTIAN
LIFE. Discourses. Cr. 8vo., 7s. 6d.

Martineau (JAMES)—*continued.*
THE SEAT OF AUTHORITY IN RELIGION.
8vo., 14s.
ESSAYS, REVIEWS, AND ADDRESSES. 4
Vols. Crown 8vo., 7s. 6d. each.
HOME PRAYERS, with Two Services for
Public Worship. Crown 8vo. 3s. 6d.

Max Müller (F.).
THE SIX SYSTEMS OF INDIAN PHIL-
OSOPHY. 8vo., 18s.
CONTRIBUTIONS TO THE SCIENCE OF
MYTHOLOGY. 2 vols. 8vo., 32s.
THE ORIGIN AND GROWTH OF RE-
LIGION, as illustrated by the Religions
of India. The Hibbert Lectures,
delivered at the Chapter House,
Westminster Abbey, in 1878. Crown
8vo., 5s.
INTRODUCTION TO THE SCIENCE OF
RELIGION : Four Lectures delivered at
the Royal Institution. Cr. 8vo., 5s.
NATURAL RELIGION. The Gifford
Lectures, delivered before the Uni-
versity of Glasgow in 1888. Cr. 8vo.,
5s.
PHYSICAL RELIGION. The Gifford
Lectures, delivered before the Uni-
versity of Glasgow in 1890. Cr. 8vo.,
5s.
ANTHROPOLOGICAL RELIGION. The Gif-
ford Lectures, delivered before the
University of Glasgow in 1891. Cr.
8vo., 5s.
THEOSOPHY ; or, PSYCHOLOGICAL RELI-
GION. The Gifford Lectures, delivered
before the University of Glasgow in
1892. Cr. 8vo., 5s.
THREE LECTURES ON THE VEDANTA
PHILOSOPHY, delivered at the Royal
Institution in March, 1894. 8vo., 5s.
RAMAKRISHNA : HIS LIFE AND SAY-
INGS. Crown 8vo., 5s.

Romanes.—THOUGHTS ON RELIGION.
By GEORGE J. ROMANES, LL.D.,
F.R.S. Crown 8vo., 4s. 6d.

Vivekananda.—YOGA PHILOSOPHY :
Lectures delivered in New York, Winter
of 1895-6, by the SWAMI VIVEKAN-
ANDA, on Raja Yoga ; or, Conquering
the Internal Nature ; also Patanjali's
Yoga Aphorisms, with Commentaries.
Crown 8vo., 3s. 6d.

Williamson. — THE GREAT LAW :
A Study of Religious Origins and of
the Unity underlying them. By W.
WILLIAMSON. 8vo., 14s.